A GUIDE TO
VIDEO GAME
MOVIES

To my mother, Patricia, and my father, Dave. We were always looked after in every way, but your love of gaming and movies passed on to us, and my passion for the entries in this book would never have ignited if it wasn't for you. I love you both.

To my big brothers, Graham and David. We experienced so many of these games and movies together, and always managed to laugh even if they were terrible. Thanks for sharing so many gaming memories with me. Love you guys.

To my wife, Dawn. You are everything to me. You're my better half, my rock and the love of my life. Without your support I could never have put this all together. Thanks for always believing in me and saying I should write about games for a living. Now you just have to listen to me talk about books every day instead. I love you more than I can ever put into words.

To Aurora, Bram and Fia. You make every day worth living. I am so proud of you all. You are the sweetest, brightest and most caring kids in the whole wide world, and being your daddy is the best thing I will ever do. Watching you grow and love and laugh and game is the most beautiful part of my life. Daddy loves you all more than anything, ever. I hope this book isn't too boring for ye...

A GUIDE TO VIDEO GAME MOVIES

Christopher Carton

WHITE OWL

AN IMPRINT OF PEN & SWORD BOOKS LTD.
YORKSHIRE – PHILADELPHIA

First published in Great Britain in 2022 by
Pen and Sword WHITE OWL
An imprint of
Pen & Sword Books Ltd
Yorkshire - Philadelphia

ISBN 978 1 39909 217 3

Typeset in 12/16 PT Sans
by SJmagic DESIGN SERVICES, India.

Printed and bound in India by Replika Press Pvt. Ltd.

Pen & Sword Books Ltd incorporates the imprints of Pen & Sword Books Archaeology, Atlas, Aviation, Battleground, Discovery, Family History, History, Maritime, Military, Naval, Politics, Railways, Select, Transport, True Crime, Fiction, Frontline Books, Leo Cooper, Praetorian Press, Seaforth Publishing, Wharncliffe and White Owl.

For a complete list of Pen & Sword titles please contact

PEN & SWORD BOOKS LIMITED
47 Church Street, Barnsley, South Yorkshire, S70 2AS, England
E-mail: enquiries@pen-and-sword.co.uk
Website: www.pen-and-sword.co.uk

or

PEN AND SWORD BOOKS
1950 Lawrence Rd, Havertown, PA 19083, USA
E-mail: Uspen-and-sword@casematepublishers.com
Website: www.penandswordbooks.com

Contents

Introduction

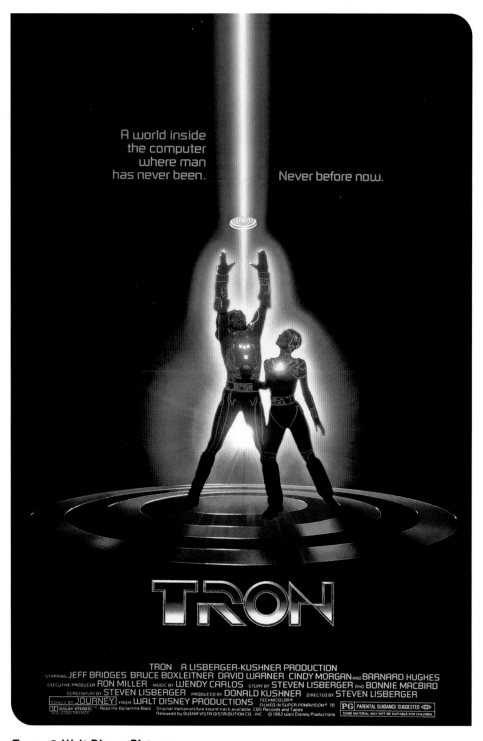

Tron – © Walt Disney Pictures

Video games and film have been linked as mediums for decades. With the advent of arcades in the '70s, gaming slowly but surely made its way into the mainstream, rising and falling in popularity as the quality and success of releases fluctuated. Arcade classics like *Space Invaders, Donkey Kong* and *Galaga* devoured the wallets of patrons, and, with the arrival of home consoles, budding gamers were able to crack their high scores from the comfort of their own homes.

From the '80s onwards, gaming made its presence felt in Hollywood and in the Japanese animation and film industry. Movies like *Tron* (1982), Disney's revolutionary digital sci-fi adventure, saw Jeff Bridges' Kevin Flynn transported into an arcade machine and onto the Grid, a digital world occupied by humanoid 'programs'. Here, he takes part in light-cycle races, disc battles and, ultimately, with the help of the eponymous program Tron, tries to save the game world from an entity known as the Master Control Program.

While this came before Hollywood decided to directly adapt gaming properties, *Tron* threw itself fully into the idea of video games as a narrative device, and along with its sequel *Tron: Legacy* (2010), have cemented themselves as cult classics and visual powerhouses.

This trend continued throughout the '80s with movies like *WarGames* (1983), the techno-thriller focused on the dark and relatively new world of computer hacking, and *The Last Starfighter* (1984), in which a young boy is recruited to fight an intergalactic war due to his video game skills.

The decade rounded out with *The Wizard* (1989), a movie about a boy whose life has been struck by tragedy, but whose skill at video games gives him a chance to take part in a tournament with a massive cash prize. Notorious for being part family adventure, part advertising vehicle for Japanese tech giant Nintendo, *The Wizard* didn't have the greatest critical reception at the time, but like a lot of misunderstood movies, it is now remembered fondly and is somewhat of a cult classic. Most importantly, it was the first introduction to the classic video game *Super Mario Bros. 3* (1990) for Western audiences, along with being Tobey Macguire's movie debut. Also, it DID feature the infamous Nintendo peripheral known as the Power Glove...

1992 saw the release of *The Lawnmower Man*, a science-fiction horror film which took its name from a short story by famed horror author Stephen King. The film contained revolutionary computer graphics, showcasing a frightening virtual world of striking imagery and terrifying danger. But as the '90s moved ahead, so too would Hollywood's interest in directly adapting video games into film form. The following are some of Hollywood's biggest attempts at successfully re-creating the video game experience on the big screen during the '90s.

Super Mario Bros.

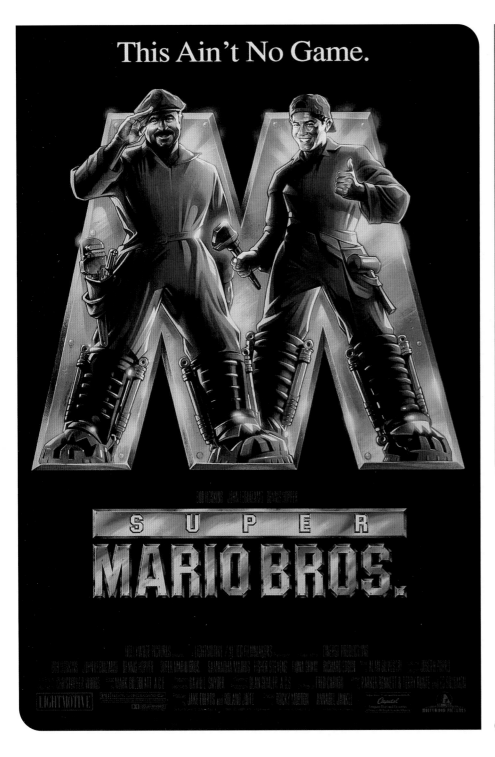

This Ain't No Game.

RELEASE DATE
28 May 1993

DIRECTORS
Rocky Morton &
Annabel Jankel

STARRING
Bob Hoskins,
John Leguizamo,
Dennis Hopper

TAGLINE
"This Ain't No
Game"

© Nintendo

I t was fitting that the first Hollywood adaptation of a video game would be based on one of the hits that revitalised the medium and brought gaming securely into the homes of millions.

With the release of the Nintendo Entertainment System (NES) in 1985, the family-friendly Japanese developer and publisher, Nintendo, had given gamers around the world an exciting new reason to play. With high-end graphics, inspired gameplay and franchises that continue to innovate and thrive to this day, the NES cemented itself as a pop culture phenomenon.

Arguably, no single game is as revered as *Super Mario Bros.*, the iconic platform game following the Italian plumber siblings as they run, jump and squash their way through the Mushroom Kingdom to defeat the evil Bowser and rescue Princess Toadstool from his clutches. The game contained tight, precise controls and innovations that would become the standard for countless games to follow. Its bright, colourful worlds and legendary music offered visuals and audio that audiences could only have dreamed of on previous systems.

The *Super Mario* series actually had a film adaptation in 1986: an animated movie with a meta storyline in which Mario and Luigi actually enter their TV in order to rescue Princess Peach. It was called *Super Mario Bros.: Peach-Hime Kyushutsu Dai Sakusen!* (The Great Mission to Rescue Princess Peach!). The Mario Bros. had made their small screen debut during the late '80s and '90s, in three separate animated series. First came *The Super Mario Bros. Super Show!* (1989), which was quickly followed by *The Adventures of Super Mario Bros. 3* (1990), and finally, *Super Mario World* (1991). When the time came for video games to make the leap to the silver screen, it must have been a no-brainer to have the famous duo suit up and lead the charge.

Super Mario Bros. for the Nintendo Entertainment System – © Nintendo

Given complete creative control by Nintendo, the crew brought forward an altogether different vision than the famous games and their animated series were known for. Gone were the chirpy, memorable tunes and the fantastical Mushroom Kingdom with its cast of cartoonish enemies. In came *Dinohattan*. The Mario brothers (Bob Hoskins and John Leguizamo) were given a Brooklyn makeover and taken on an inter-dimensional adventure to a dystopian, cyberpunk world complete with sleazy criminals, Blade Runner-esque neon cityscapes and established actors chewing the scenery at every turn.

"Trust the fungus!"

– Luigi Mario (John Leguizamo)

This drastic change to the source material proved to be a love/hate scenario, with the late Bob Hoskins once describing it as a 'nightmare' and the worst thing he ever did. However, the film has gone on to become somewhat of a cult classic, moving up in many people's estimations for its surreal tone, campy humour, bizarre yet intriguing character designs and a myriad of practical special effects and animatronics. It's also chock-full of references for eagle-eyed fans to find, such as a bar named after the enemy 'Bullet Bill', a tiny, wind up Bob-omb, and an eerily realistic Yoshi.

Dennis Hopper is a particularly over-the-top President Koopa, spouting grandiose plans as he paces about the vast, cold sets. Joining him in his villainy are veteran actors Fiona Shaw (the *Harry Potter* series) as Lena, Richard Edson (*Howard the Duck, Platoon*) as Spike, and Oscar winner Fisher Stevens (the *Short Circuit* series, *Lost*) as Iggy. These baddies attempt to thwart, deceive and destroy the Mario brothers at every turn, throwing lightning-quick one-liners and slapstick into the mix at every opportunity.

A Goomba, one of King Koopa's minions. – © Nintendo

Luigi Mario (John Leguizamo) and Mario Mario (Bob Hoskins) – © Nintendo

The film remains a significant adaptation in the gaming world, and it certainly set the tone for the rollercoaster ride that would be Hollywood's relationship with video games going forward.

WATCH IT FOR

There are plenty of reasons to catch this flick, but a standout moment is a scene in which Mario and Luigi get trapped inside an elevator with the movie's version of the Goomba enemies, who are giant, but dim-witted, creatures. Mario and Luigi distract them by getting them to sway and dance to the lift's jolly tune in a surreal moment from this sci-fi adventure.

SEQUEL?

Not exactly, but Illumination, the animation studio behind *Despicable Me, Minions* and *The Grinch* are currently working on an animated version of *Super Mario* that will surely be much closer to the games in tone and look.

There was a sequel webcomic produced in 2013, in conjunction with one of the film's screenwriters, Parker Bennett. In it, Mario and Luigi returned to Dinohattan to help Daisy on a new quest, which was hinted at with the movie's cliffhanger ending.

A new cut of the movie surfaced online in mid-2021, with nearly half an hour of extra footage.

Double Dragon

RELEASE DATE
4 November 1994

DIRECTOR
James Yukich

STARRING
Scott Wolf, Mark Dacascos, Robert Patrick

TAGLINE
"Power. Justice. Darkness. Light."

© Gramercy Pictures

Double Dragon II: The Revenge – © Arc System Works

It only took a year for Hollywood to turn its hand to a new adaptation of a classic video game franchise. The *Double Dragon* series began in 1987 with the arcade original – a side-scrolling beat 'em up that was a huge hit with players worldwide. This version was ported to the NES and various other systems in the decades that followed.

Players took control of twin brothers Billy and Jimmy Lee as they traversed goon-filled streets and did battle with the Black Warriors gang, hoping to save their mutual romantic interest, a woman named Marian. The game is credited with many staples of the genre: using crude, street weaponry to defeat enemies, deadly verticality to test players' platforming skills, and punishing boss fights that are sure to lose you a life or two. Titles such as *Final Fight* and the *Streets of Rage* series owe a lot to the action-packed adventures of the Lee brothers.

The film oozes a distinct '90s aesthetic in every facet of its design. With a colour palette resembling bags of Skittles thrown into a ball pit, dialogue so cheesy it makes the strongest blue cheese seem like mild cheddar, and a villainous Robert Patrick who wouldn't look out of place as a George Michael impersonator, *Double Dragon* is playful, ridiculous fun. The martial arts work here is authentic and impressive and the chemistry between Scott Wolf (Billy) and Mark Dacascos (Jimmy) is undeniable.

Alyssa Milano plays Marian, in this instance changed from her damsel-in-distress role to the leader of a group of vigilantes known as the Power Corps. She aids the brothers in their quest to stop evil

Jimmy Lee (Mark Dacascos), Marian Delario (Alyssa Milano) and Billy Lee (Scott Wolf) – © Gramercy Pictures

Koga Shuko (Robert
Patrick) –
© Gramercy Pictures

crime lord Koga Shuko (Robert Patrick) from acquiring both halves of the Double Dragon amulet. Through their mentor Satori Imada (Julia Nickson) and her teachings, the brothers must learn how to work together and fight with honour to take down Shuko and his goons. Filled with set pieces and suitably light-hearted jokes, the movie is a zippy experience that rushes towards its climax.

> "My whole life just flashed before my eyes! Dude, I sleep a lot."
> – Billy Lee (Scott Wolf)

Along the way, there is an action scene on a river, filmed in Ohio, which culminates with an explosion. The blast was so immense that it caused disruption for a nearby town, and emergency services were notified due to the concern of residents.

Mixing the gritty and uninviting crime-riddled alleys of a *RoboCop* movie with family-friendly hijinks and impressive stunt work, *Double Dragon* continued the trend of outlandish and over-the-top adaptations of video games.

WATCH IT FOR

Robert Patrick is as ludicrously cartoonish as a villain can be, and his performance in this movie – a far cry from the menacing T-1000 in *Terminator 2: Judgment Day* (1992) – is worth your time alone.

SEQUEL?

No sequel ever came for this family-friendly martial arts flick. However, a video game which followed in 1995 contained anime-influenced versions of many of the film's characters, as well as featuring Marian in her role as a heroine, and Koga Shuko, who had been created specifically for the film. Unlike the main series, this game was a one-on-one fighting game similar to *Street Fighter* and *Mortal Kombat*.

Street Fighter

RELEASE DATE
23 December 1994

DIRECTOR
Steven E. de Souza

STARRING
Jean-Claude
Van Damme,
Raul Julia,
Kylie Minogue

TAGLINE
"The Ultimate
Battle"

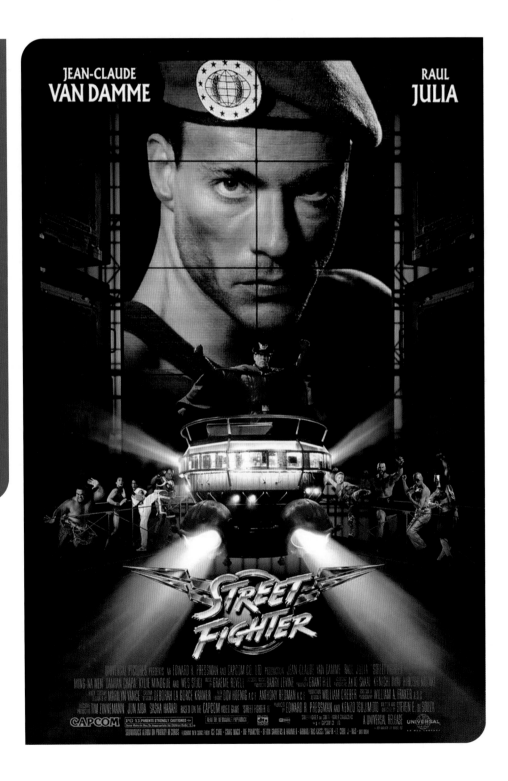

Street Fighter II was a mega-hit that took the world by storm – first in arcades, then in the homes of console owners. With its colourful, enticing world, addictive and satisfying gameplay and stellar soundtrack, it was released for the SNES and Mega Drive/Genesis and re-released in various forms for decades after its initial street date.

At the height of its popularity, Capcom optioned a film adaptation, giving gamers and movie-goers alike a chance to see the bone-crunching battles of legendary characters such as Ryu, Guile, Chun-Li and the tough-as-nails final boss and big bad, the villainous M. Bison, play out on the big screen (It was preceded earlier that same year by *Street Fighter II: The Movie*, which was an anime adaptation that recreated the game's events in a more traditional way).

Set in the fictional Asian war-torn country of Shadaloo, it follows Colonel William Guile and his army's attempt to liberate the country from a powerful dictator known as M. Bison. Bison here is played by the late Raul Julia, fresh off his hilarious and captivating role as Gomez Addams in both *The Addams Family* and its sequel, *Addams Family Values*. Sadly, Julia died before *Street Fighter*'s release, and the movie is dedicated to his memory, as the end credits read "For Raul. Via Con Dios", honouring the actor's Puerto Rican heritage.

"Now, who wants to go home... and who wants to go with ME!?"
– Colonel William Guile (Jean-Claude Van Damme)

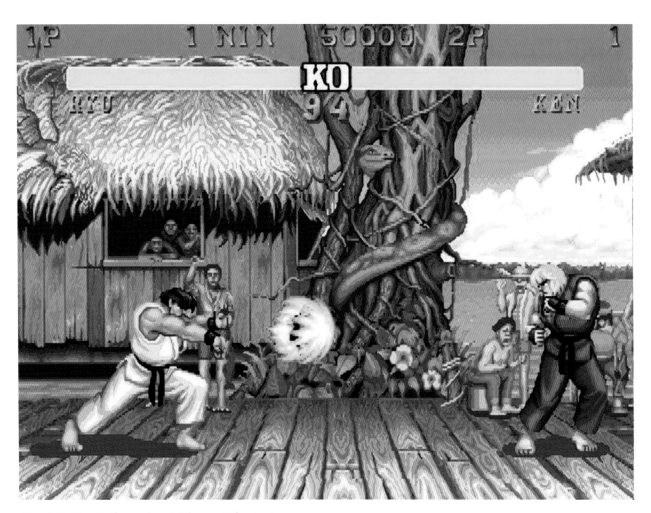

Street Fighter II: Champion Edition – © Capcom

What a final role it would turn out to be. Regardless of your experience with the *Street Fighter* franchise, this movie is a thick slice of silly, quotable '90s action. Jean-Claude Van Damme plays Guile, and he is intent on owning any scene he is in with his over-the-top, bombastic proclamations and several monologues purpose-built to rouse the soldiers he fights with into action against Bison and his cronies. The movie is absolutely filled to the brim with characters from *Street Fighter II*.

Fans can enjoy the comical, yet menacing Zangief, the loveable and powerful E. Honda, the iconic Chun-Li and even a big-screen version of the vicious Blanka, here given a torturous origin story that also involves a loose interpretation of the stretchy Hindu yoga master Dhalsim. The film moves at break-neck speed, giving plenty of time for both intentionally and unintentionally hilarious moments as well as numerous references to the video game.

Ming-Na Wen portrays Chun-Li, a news reporter caught in the fray of the Shadaloo warzone, along with her friends Edmond Honda and former boxer, Balrog. As Chun-Li seeks out Bison for the murder of her father, the trio join Guile, Ryu and Ken in their battle for justice. This sets up plenty of epic fights that play out as if they were straight from the game itself. Of particular note is Vega, the masked Spanish fighter with deadly claws which he uses to attack his enemies, and whose entrance takes place in a ring surrounded by a cage and a cheering crowd, just like his stage from the video game.

Bison's floating craft is controlled using the lollipop-shaped control stick and chunky buttons of an authentic arcade cabinet, and as American con men and series staples Ryu and Ken are brought into Bison's ranks by his right-hand man, Zangief, they don their iconic white and red robes. Kylie Minogue's Cammy is a fairly accurate representation of her video game counterpart, showing her fighting skills as well as her sense of justice and will to do what is right.

Street Fighter was almost entirely financed by the developer, Capcom, and they were said to have had a hand in many of its design choices and the overall direction of the movie. It didn't fare well with critics, but like the previous '90s movies, it has garnered cult status.

Dee Jay (Miguel A. Núñez Jr.), M. Bison (Raul Juila) and Zangief (Andrew Bryniarski) – © Capcom & Colombia TriStar Film Distributors International

The heroes of *Street Fighter*, in their victory poses. – © Capcom & Colombia TriStar Film Distributors International

WATCH IT FOR

Everything. Nostalgia, if you've seen it, disbelief and hopefully loads of belly laughs if you haven't, and mainly for the brilliant performance by Raul Julia as M. Bison. It's almost guaranteed to put a smile on your face.

SEQUEL?

No direct sequel was made for this iteration. However, an animated *Street Fighter* series followed that borrowed some elements from the Shadaloo adventure. Digitised versions of the actors in the movie were used in two different releases of *Street Fighter: The Movie* – one for arcades and another for the PlayStation and Sega Saturn. A reboot followed in 2009, called *Street Fighter: The Legend of Chun-Li,* with Kristin Kreuk (*Smallville*) playing the title character. A live-action miniseries called *Street Fighter: Assassin's Fist* was released in 2014. It is a canonical origin story for Ryu and Ken and it was well-received by fans and critics.

Mortal Kombat

RELEASE DATE
18 August 1995

DIRECTOR
Paul W.S. Anderson

STARRING
Robin Shou,
Christopher
Lambert,
Cary-Hiroyuki
Tagawa

TAGLINE
"NOTHING IN
THIS WORLD HAS
PREPARED YOU
FOR THIS"

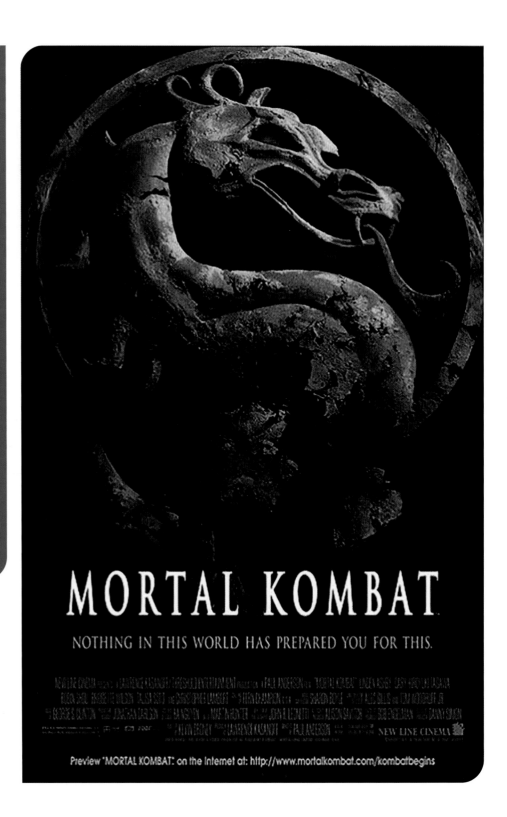

Few games have garnered the controversy that the *Mortal Kombat* series has. Along with the full-motion video horror-adventure game *Night Trap,* it was synonymous with the creation of the ESRB (Entertainment Software Rating Board), which still controls the age rating of gaming in the United States. *Mortal Kombat* drew its share of acclaim and criticism: the former for its stellar photo-realistic, digitised characters and intricate one-on-one gameplay, the latter aimed at its gratuitous violence, especially in its infamous 'Fatalities'. These finishing moves brought the violence to a new level, with scalded bodies, decapitations and impalement on massive spikes, to name a few.

Warriors such as Liu Kang, Kano, Johnny Cage, Raiden and the mighty sorcerer Shang Tsung did battle across a variety of dark fantasy settings, wielding spectacular special moves, inspired visual designs and gruesome finishers. The foreboding atmosphere of Shang Tsung's island, the game's setting, was a perfect fit for these tense and epic fights.

"Your soul is MINE!!"

– Shang Tsung (Cary-Hiroyuki Tagawa)

It proved to be a massive success on a multitude of platforms, including the SNES (where the blood was replaced with 'sweat' in an effort to lower the violent content), the Mega Drive/ Genesis, the Game Boy and Game Gear, the Sega CD, the Amiga and PC. Its popularity was due in no small part to the taboo nature of the violence it portrayed, although critical praise was near-unanimous for the gameplay. Owing to its popularity and infamy, Hollywood saw its opportunity to bring the gothic, fantastical battles of *Mortal Kombat* to the big screen. Enlisting Paul W.S. Anderson, a man who would go on to direct no less than five more video game adaptations, *Mortal Kombat* exploded onto screens in 1995 following massive anticipation.

The movie itself is a fast-paced adventure, made accessible through the chemistry of its leads. Liu Kang, Sonya Blade and Johnny Cage, amongst others, travel to the sorcerer Shang Tsung's island to take part in Mortal Kombat, a tournament designed to win Earthrealm its

Mortal Kombat –
© Warner Bros.
Interactive
Entertainment

Shang Tsung (Cary-Hiroyuki Tagawa) – © New Line Cinema Liu Kang (Robin Shou) – © New Line Cinema

freedom from Outworld, an evil alternate world ruled by the malevolent emperor, Shao Khan. The film follows the plot of the original game fairly closely, including staples such as Sub-Zero, Scorpion, Reptile and Kitana, the last of whom aids the heroes in their quest to topple their enemies.

Mortal Kombat has an interesting visual style, with effects that were extremely impressive for the time. The hulking, four-armed champion Goro still looks massively imposing even today, and the now legendary *Techno Syndrome* by The Immortals is one of the most recognisable film theme tunes of all time. It's one part of a pulse-pounding techno soundtrack that fits the fast-paced martial arts on screen perfectly.

The on-screen adventures of Earthrealm's heroes, led by the thunder god Rayden (or "Raiden" in the video games - Christopher Lambert), proved to be a massive success at the box office, and its impact is still felt to this day. The most recent entry in the gaming series, *Mortal Kombat 11* (2019 – PS4, Xbox One, Nintendo Switch, Google Stadia, Steam; 2020 – PS5, Xbox Series S/X) included some of the movie's characters as downloadable content, starting with Shang Tsung, and later following up with Johnny Cage, Sonya Blade and Rayden. All four character skins feature the likenesses and voices of the actors who portrayed them in this film.

WATCH IT FOR

The sets, the martial arts and the stellar soundtrack. While it may not have much of the gore of the video games, *Mortal Kombat* is atmospheric, quotable and genuinely funny.

SEQUEL?

Yes. Given the massive box office success of Anderson's film, the first live-action video game adaptation sequel went into production and was released two years later. It was called *Mortal Kombat: Annihilation*.

Mortal Kombat: Annihilation

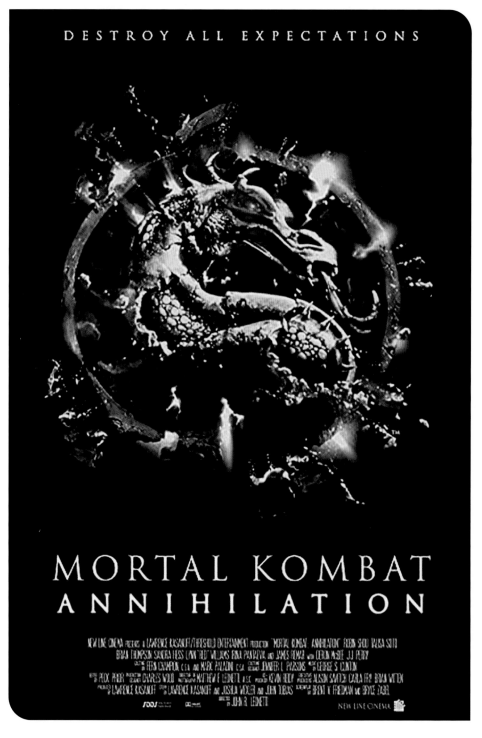

RELEASE DATE
21 November 1997

DIRECTOR
John R. Leonetti

STARRING
Robin Shou, James Remar, Brian Thompson

TAGLINE
"Destroy All Expectations"

Expectations were destroyed, but probably not in the way many were expecting. The only two actors who returned for this fantasy-action sequel were Robin Shou (Liu Kang) and Talisa Soto (Kitana). While Liu Kang's remaining allies all continued to battle, they were now portrayed by new actors, including James Remar (*The Warriors, Dexter*) as Rayden.

> "Mother! You're alive!"
>
> – Kitana (Talisa Soto)

> "Too bad YOU...will die!!"
>
> – Sindel (Musetta Vander)

Even though the heroes had seemingly saved Earthrealm from a dark fate, the Emperor Shao Khan declares his plan to subject the earth to annihilation, a merging of Earthrealm and Outworld, regardless of the outcome of the tournament. Given a timeframe of six days before the malevolent leader goes through with his plans, the heroes of Earthrealm set out across the grim and desolate Outworld to find allies to aid them in their quest.

Mortal Kombat: Annihilation, like 1994's *Street Fighter* before it, is intent on cramming as many recognisable characters as possible into its sub-two-hour run time. Based primarily on the video game *Mortal Kombat 3* (1995 – Mega Drive/Genesis, SNES, PlayStation, Game Boy, Game Gear, Master System, PC), the journey across the realm packs in the cyborgs Noob-Saibot (named after the game series creators Ed Boon and John Tobias), Cyrax, Goro's female counterpart Sheeva, Sonya's old partner Jax (here recast from the original movie) and the horrific, razor-toothed Baraka. Sub-Zero returns, although he is the brother of the character from the 1995 original, and an ally of Liu Kang and Kitana.

The film has more in common with *Power Rangers* or a Saturday morning cartoon than the darker tone of the original. That's not to say that the 1995 movie is rife with deep, Shakespearean dialogue, but this sequel moves from set piece to set piece with little to no introduction for

Mortal Kombat 3 –
© **Warner Bros. Interactive Entertainment**

The heroes of *Mortal Kombat: Annihilation* – © New Line Cinema

The villains of *Mortal Kombat: Annihilation* – © New Line Cinema

many of the characters. They're here solely to fight, which is in keeping with the spirit of the early games, at least. Front flips (including a completely bizarre and unnecessarily dramatic one by Brian Thompson's Shao Khan as he leaves his throne to speak with his father, Shinnok) and diagonal camera shots are in plentiful supply in this movie, as is PlayStation 1 level CG effects and more techno than you can shake a severed spine at.

Ultimately, *Mortal Kombat: Annihilation* was poorly received by fans and critics alike. Series creator Ed Boon once named it as his least favourite thing in the franchise. It should be commended for its enthusiasm, and there are surely some elements in it that fans of the original will enjoy. If you wanted more high-flying martial arts and desolate landscapes, this movie more than delivers.

WATCH IT FOR

The flood of classic MK characters. From Nightwolf to Shinnok to Baraka, this movie is intent on providing as much fan service as it does cheesy dialogue.

SEQUEL?

Due to the disappointing reception of *Annihilation*, a third in this series never materialised, although it was initially planned. The next time *Mortal Kombat* would show up on film would be in 2010, when Kevin Tancharoen directed a short film called *Mortal Kombat: Rebirth*. The idea behind this project was a pitch to Warner Bros. for a potential new movie in the franchise. Instead, Tancharoen followed this up with the web series *Mortal Kombat: Legacy*, which premiered in 2013 and had two seasons, with a mostly positive reception. In Season 2, Cary-Hiroyuki Tagawa played the menacing sorcerer Shang Tsung once again.

An animated movie, *Mortal Kombat Legends: Scorpion's Revenge* was released on home video in 2020, and it follows Scorpion as he seeks to avenge his fallen family.

A new *Mortal Kombat* film, eponymously titled, released on 23 April 2021 and was directed by Simon McQuoid. It featured a new cast, a storyline unconnected to the previous movies and hyper-violence akin to the video game franchise. A second animated movie, *Mortal Kombat Legends: Battle of the Realms*, was released in August 2021.

Wing Commander

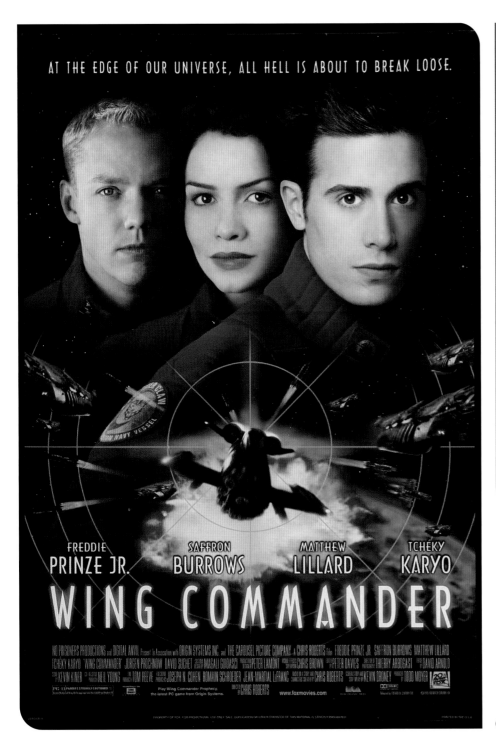

© 20th Century Fox

RELEASE DATE
12 March 1999

DIRECTOR
Chris Roberts

STARRING
Freddie Prinze Jr.,
Matthew Lillard,
Saffron Burrows

TAGLINE
"At the Edge of
Our Universe, All
Hell is About to
Break Loose"

Wing Commander wowed the gaming world in 1990. An incredibly in-depth space simulator, it featured thrilling dog fights, superb graphics and a dynamic storyline which altered its course depending on player skill and choices. While previous movie adaptations built on the fairly sparse narrative seeds of the games on which they were based, Wing Commander and its sequels had storylines rivalling that of many Hollywood movies.

Players took control of the then-unnamed Christopher Blair; a blue-haired, level-headed fighter pilot in the midst of the war between Earth and the Kilrathi, a humanoid-feline species bent on universal domination. Blair was later portrayed by veteran actor Mark Hamill in *Wing Commander III* & *Wing Commander IV*, the latter of which featured revolutionary, live-action cutscenes interspersed with the gameplay. Blair's superhuman powers as a 'Pilgrim' offer him battle insight with acute senses and instincts, but likewise can often bring unwarranted, negative attention to his actions.

> "My whole life I've taken crap because I'm part Pilgrim. And I don't know why..."
> – Christopher Blair (Freddie Prinze Jr.)

The man behind the creative direction of the gaming series, Chris Roberts, was the obvious choice to take the helm on a movie adaptation of the revolutionary space opera. The lead character, Christopher Blair, was once again the focus when it came to the silver screen, but this time he was portrayed by Freddie Prinze Jr. (*I Know What You Did Last Summer, Star Wars Rebels, She's All That*). He was joined by Matthew Lillard (*Scream, Th13teen Ghosts,* the *Scooby-Doo* series) as Todd 'Maniac' Marshall, another first lieutenant who, along with Blair, travels under Captain James Taggart (Tcheky Karyo – *The Missing, Kiss of the Dragon*) on a mission to reach their new post, the Tiger Claw.

Wing Commander –
© **Electronic Arts**

Christopher Blair (Freddie Prinze Jr.) – © 20th Century Fox

Blair deals with his own legacy, one that seems oddly familiar to the Captain, but doesn't sit well with some of his commanding officers. Together, the ragtag crew throw themselves into vicious dogfights with the deadly Kilrathi as they try to figure out the best way to outsmart the invading fleet.

Taking its cues as much from the *Star Wars* and *Star Trek* film series as the game franchise it's based on, *Wing Commander* attempts to recreate the exciting space warfare that garnered the many installments of the video games such acclaim. It could be argued that there was no better person to direct proceedings than the man behind the games themselves, but *Wing Commander* came out at the end of a decade filled with plenty of science fiction heavy hitters, such as *Independence Day* and *Armageddon*. While the film is visually impressive (given its modest budget) for the most part and should provide viewers with a quick fix of heroic space battles, it was poorly received by critics and was the only film Roberts has directed to date.

It didn't taint *Wing Commander*'s legacy however, as the game series had more installments following the film's release, and the original games remain a pioneering force in gaming history.

The Kilrathi – © 20th Century Fox

WATCH IT FOR

The genuine comradery between Prinze Jr. and Lillard, the Kilrathi character design, and because it has direct input by the creator of the game franchise.

SEQUEL?

No. Given the poor critical reception and a box office take that was only a third of its budget, it's unsurprising that *Wing Commander* never saw a sequel.

Pokémon – The First Movie: Mewtwo Strikes Back

RELEASE DATE
18 July 1998

DIRECTOR
Kunihiko Yuyama

STARRING THE VOICES OF
Veronica Taylor, Ikue Ōtani, Philip Bartlett

TAGLINE
"Who is the strongest Pokémon!?"

With the release of *Pokémon Red & Blue* and the anime series that followed, the pocket monster franchise had reached global fame, entrancing millions of players and viewers around the world. The adventures of Ash Ketchum (from Pallet Town!) and his friends Misty and Brock, brought colourful life to the Kanto region and its 150 species of Pokémon.

A film version of Pokémon was inevitable and, when it did arrive, it needed to raise the stakes from the weekly series that saw Ash, along with his close companion Pikachu, on a journey across the region to battle their way to see Ash become a Pokémon master. The movie sees the main trio and the iconic electric mouse return, this time being invited to a competition on a mysterious landmass called 'New Island'.

> "We do have a lot in common: the same Earth, the same air, the same sky. Maybe, if we started looking at what's the same instead of what's different, well... who knows?"
>
> – Mewtwo (Philip Bartlett)

Behind the invitation is the mysterious Mewtwo, a laboratory creation given life using D.N.A. from the rarest known Pokémon, Mew. Brought to consciousness in confusion and captivity, with a limited number of friends with which to share his feelings, Mewtwo breaks free, causing chaos in the process. His existence fragile and his heart filled with hatred, he hatches a plan to gather unsuspecting trainers so that he can clone their Pokémon to be his loyal companions.

This movie is perfect for fans of the cartoon series, as it follows the winning formula of Indigo League – the first iteration of the cartoon series – authentically. With light-hearted moments from the ever-bumbling Team Rocket and their chatterbox Pokémon, Meowth, plenty of intense Pokémon battles and the always heart-warming friendship between Ash and Pikachu, it feels like an extended episode of the TV show, which is surely enough for most fans.

Moving to a new setting helps the movie feel bigger in a sense, although the animation is fairly typical of the show. The voice acting is energetic and helps to give the characters a real sense of life, particularly Philip Bartlett as Mewtwo, who gives the sympathetic villain real emotion as

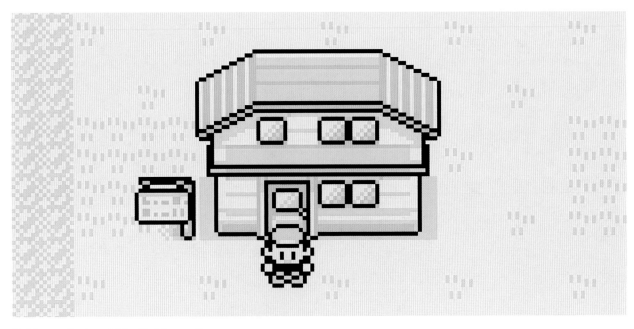

Pokémon Red – © The Pokémon Company

Above: **Pikachu and Ash – © The Pokémon Company**

Right: **Mewtwo – © The Pokémon Company**

he struggles to figure out his role in a world where he doesn't belong.

Unsurprisingly, the movie was a massive success, grossing millions around the world. It didn't fare well with critics, but seeing as it was made to cater to fans, the reception from them was much better.

WATCH IT FOR

The genuinely moving story around Mewtwo, the battles between Pokémon and their clone versions, and a new version of the classic theme song that plays over the opening credits.

SEQUEL?

Yes. Like the anime and the video games, the movie series continued, and 22 more animated Pokémon films have been released to date. One of these is a fully computer-generated remake of *The First Movie*, called *Pokémon: Mewtwo Strikes Back – Evolution* (2019).

Pokémon also made the leap to live-action with the 2019 movie, *Pokémon – Detective Pikachu*.

The Best of the Rest – '90s

While these adaptations comprised Hollywood's first decade of attempts at bringing successful video games to another medium, many other projects, both high-profile and niche, were released from other territories in the form of TV movies and straight-to-video releases.

Japanese developer SNK had three of their popular fighting series given screen treatment in the early '90s in the form of anime movies. *Fatal Fury* saw three installments. *Fatal Fury: Legend of the Hungry Wolf* (1992) and *Fatal Fury 2: The New Battle* (1993) arrived first, both of which see the Bogard brothers, Terry and Andy, in their martial arts-filled quests to defeat crime bosses Geese Howard and Wolfgang Krauser, and avenge the death of their father in the process. They were followed by *Fatal Fury: The Motion Picture* in 1994. The anime film once again features the Bogard brothers and other series staples, but simultaneously introduces new, original characters.

Samurai Shodown: The Movie arrived in 1994, loosely adapting the first game in the feudal Japan era one-on-one fighting game franchise. *Art of Fighting* also got its own anime movie in 1993, although it was poorly received compared to other similar releases of that time. SNK's *Fatal Fury* and *Art of Fighting* series share the same universe, and characters from both would later be gathered into the hugely successful and long-running *King of Fighters* series.

A 1991 anime movie version of Tecmo's classic run-and-slash series *Ninja Gaiden* was released, and it dealt with the deadly ninja Ryu Hayabusa and his battles with conjured demons. Various short films were released in this decade too, such as *Dragonball Z Side Story: Plan to Eradicate the Saiyans* (1993), which is an adaptation of the card-battling game of the same name, and two shorts based on the Square Enix tactical role-playing series *Front Mission* – (*Front Mission* in 1994 and *Front Mission Series: Gun Hazard* in 1995).

In 1995, to tie in with the live-action *Mortal Kombat* film, a semi-prequel animated film called *Mortal Kombat: The Journey Begins* was released. Using both traditional animation and computer-generated sequences, it follows Rayden as he divulges to Liu Kang, Sonya and Johnny Cage several backstories and other information about Shang Tsung and his various fighters. The '90s continued to pump out *Mortal Kombat* content, as a poorly-received animated show *Mortal Kombat: Defenders of the Realm* (1996, 1 season) and a live-action prequel series to the films, *Mortal Kombat: Conquest* (1998–1999, 1 season) were produced.

In 1996, the PlayStation and Sega Saturn fighting series *Battle Arena Toshinden* was adapted into an anime movie of the same name that mostly followed the storyline of the game *Battle Arena Toshinden 2* (1995). In that same year, one of gaming's most iconic characters, *Sonic the Hedgehog*, was given his own two-part anime series that would later be re-edited into a feature-length film. It follows Sonic, Tails and Knuckles as they battle the nefarious Dr. Robotnik on the world of Planet Freedom. It was mostly well received by critics.

Namco's one-on-one arcade fighting series *Tekken* was adapted into a two-part anime, which was combined in the west to become *Tekken: The Motion Picture* (1998). It was based on the original *Tekken* game along with some characters and elements from *Tekken 2* and *Tekken 3*. It was not well received.

At the end of the decade, Rockstar Games released a live-action short film to their website, called *GTA 2 – The Movie*, based on their blockbuster series *Grand Theft Auto*. It was uploaded to promote the release of the second installment in the series, *Grand Theft Auto 2* (1999/2000 – PlayStation, Dreamcast, Game Boy Color, PC). It featured a character called Claude Speed, and saw him doing odd jobs around the city for questionable characters, much like the game series itself.

With the advent of more powerful, fully 3D gaming in the mid-nineties (PlayStation, Sega Saturn, Nintendo 64), filmmakers set their sights on more ambitious projects that sought to bring that narrative diversity to film, while simultaneously honouring the games they were based on. The next decade would see a flood of video game movies as the relationship between the mediums continued to grow.

Lara Croft: Tomb Raider

RELEASE DATE
15 June 2001

DIRECTOR
Simon West

STARRING
Angelina Jolie, Jon Voight, Daniel Craig

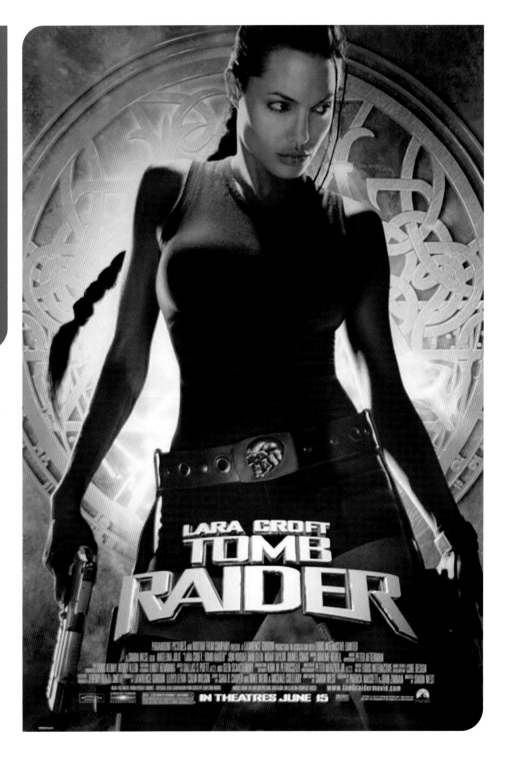

LARA CROFT: TOMB RAIDER

With the switch to full polygonal 3D, video games had reached new levels of depth, both in their design and their narratives. Full-motion video helped cutscenes to stand out with a cinematic flair, allowing for more meaningful stories, convincing voice acting and atmospheric presentation.

Tomb Raider was a breakout success for the Sega Saturn and the PlayStation. Players took on the role of a wealthy archaeologist and adventurer, Lara Croft. Throughout the '90s, Lara featured in four *Tomb Raider* games (the fifth, *Tomb Raider: Chronicles*, was released in 2000) and became a pop culture icon in her own right, even taking part in the memorable 'Larazade' advertising campaign for the energy drink brand, Lucozade.

With successful games in the public domain and her status only growing and pushing further into the mainstream, it was inevitable that Lara Croft would make her debut on film sooner rather than later. Angelina Jolie was chosen for the role, and the movie was released in 2001.

"Right... so... pretty much, touch anything and you get your head chopped off."

– Lara Croft (Angelina Jolie)

Story-wise, the movie tries its best to retain the elements that makes the game series so popular. With Croft Manor, Lara is given a training playground to hone her physical skills, aided by her butler Hillary (Chris Barrie – *Red Dwarf, Spitting Image, The Brittas Empire*) and her tech guru Bryce (Noah Taylor – *Peaky Blinders, Charlie and the Chocolate Factory, Preacher*).

Tomb Raider – © **Square Enix**

Lara Croft (Angelina Jolie) – © Paramount Pictures

With a solar eclipse looming, Lara is thrown into mysterious circumstances linked to her late father, and she's soon the target of Mandred Powell (Iain Glen – *Game of Thrones, Jack Taylor, Titans*), who is ruthlessly pursuing the parts of a triangular artifact of great power and importance. A globe-trotting adventure ensues, with Lara attempting to outwit and outpace Powell and his goons.

Mandred Powell (Iain Glen) – © Paramount Pictures

From her athletic flips, dual-wielding pistols and iconic posh British accent, Lara Croft is realised well on screen by Jolie, and her chemistry with Hillary and Bryce makes the early parts of the movie really enjoyable. Daniel Craig also supports as fellow adventurer Alex West, who has a history with Lara that fills their encounters with an unspoken tension. Alex makes his appearance several times throughout Lara's adventure, a ghost from her past she doesn't seem to be able to shake off.

While most of the games saw Lara exploring ancient ruins and deadly, booby-trapped tombs on her own, allowing players to immerse themselves in the atmosphere, the movie tends to have someone tagging along with her more often than not. This is obviously an alteration for film that allows for dialogue and one-liners to keep the audience entertained, and it highlights one of the fundamental differences in the medium of movies versus video games. When players are inherently in control, there is less pressure to bombard them with exposition. In translating this to a mostly passive form of media (beyond heated discussion or running commentaries) Lara's journey does lose some of its claustrophobic bite.

Nevertheless, it's clear the movie comes from a place of reverence for the character. Lara keeps her sarcastic confidence, her astounding athletic ability and her lust for adventure. This film version also allows for more exploration of Lara's backstory, particularly her relationship with her late father, which adds some emotional substance to the proceedings.

The movie had a mixed reception but was a huge success.

WATCH IT FOR

The emotional story, the chemistry between Lara, Hillary and Bryce, and the action-packed choreography and set pieces.

SEQUEL?

Yes. Given the box office take of the first film, a sequel followed in 2003. *Lara Croft: Tomb Raider – The Cradle of Life* saw Angelina Jolie return and put renowned action director Jan de Bont at the helm.

Final Fantasy: The Spirits Within

RELEASE DATE
11 July 2001

DIRECTOR
Hironobu
Sakaguchi

**STARRING THE
VOICES OF**
Ming-Na Wen,
Alec Baldwin,
James Woods

TAGLINE
"UNLEASH A
NEW REALITY"

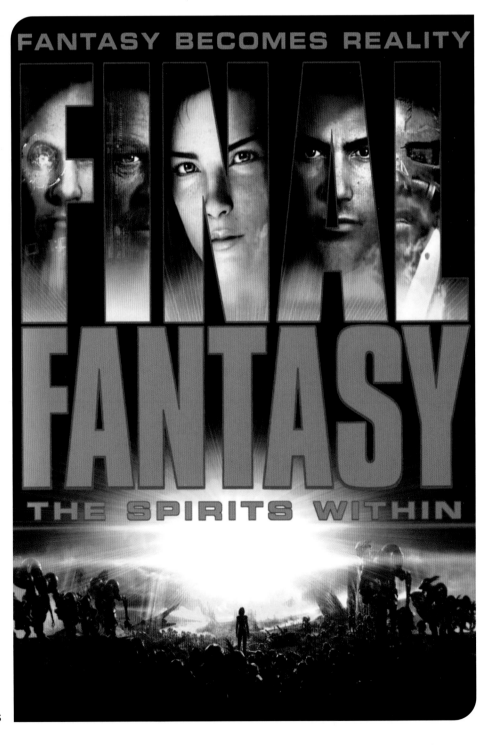

© Colombia Pictures

I t was always going to be tough bringing a franchise like *Final Fantasy* to the big screen. Each installment of the mainline series of games contains a completely different setting, scenario and cast of characters. While the initial games focused on a more classic, trope-heavy style of fantasy involving crystals, prophesied warriors, looming castles and mages adventuring through dark forests on epic quests, *Final Fantasy VI* started a more modern trend of sci-fi fantasy, blending futuristic machinery and technology with traditional swords and sorcery.

The first title to get an official release in European territories was *Final Fantasy VII*, a classic cyberpunk adventure that spanned three discs on Sony's PlayStation in 1997. Featuring beloved characters, the renowned 'Materia' system and a story and soundtrack that are still revered to this day, it brought the *Final Fantasy* series to a whole new legion of fans and had a massive part in making it the success it is today. In March 2020, the first section of the game was fully remade for the PlayStation 4 and dubbed *Final Fantasy VII Remake*, to critical acclaim. It was later expanded upon in 2021 with *Final Fantasy VII Remake – Intergrade* for PlayStation 5, which added visual upgrades and a new story involving Yuffie, a character from the original *Final Fantasy VII*.

While the eighth and ninth installments were also hugely popular, it was *FFVII*'s breakthrough that kickstarted the production of a movie adaptation of *Final Fantasy*. The man responsible for the creation of the game series, Hironobu Sakaguchi, took to the director's chair to helm what was considered one of the most visually revolutionary films ever made at the time of release. Created entirely using computer graphics and a photorealistic style, it sought to blur the lines of animation and realism and tell a brand-new story with emotional heft.

> "I told her that she wasn't dying, just returning to the Earth's spirit, to Gaia. She told me that she was ready to die. She said I didn't have to make up stories to make her feel better. Only seven years old and ready to die..."
>
> – Dr. Aki Ross (Ming-Na Wen)

Like the game series, the movie uses a new setting and characters, with only a few narrative links. The movie makes multiple references to Gaia – or the planet's life force – a similar

Cloud and a Shinra reactor in *Final Fantasy VII* – © Square Enix

plot device used in *Final Fantasy VII*, where the evil Shinra Corporation are using massive reactors to drain 'mako' energy directly from the planet's life force. It also contains a character called Sid (voiced by veteran actor Donald Sutherland), a tradition which has run through every game in the series, although the game character is known as Cid. The Cid characters in the video games are usually older than the core cast, and technically minded and wise. This is the case in the movie also, as Dr. Sid is helping the main character, Dr. Aki Ross (Ming-Na Wen), search for spirits: entities which can aid in a defence against invading phantoms.

Set in a post-apocalyptic Earth, the phantoms have ravaged most of the major cities of the world. These ghostly creatures have the ability to steal human life with a single touch, pulling their victims spirits from their bodies and ending their lives. Aki and a small band of soldiers known as Deep Eyes eventually team up and, with Dr. Sid's help, they begin to search for spirits which he believes will 'heal' the planet and end the invasion of the phantoms.

Those looking for a traditional *Final Fantasy* experience might be disappointed at the direction the film took. In place of a sword and magic approach, the film delves into full-on science fiction, and maintains a fairly dark tone for the majority of its run-time. Steve Buscemi's character, Neil, does provide some comic relief with his often ill-timed one-liners, but other than that the movie remains desolate and eerie. Sakaguchi often associated *Final Fantasy* with the evolution of technology, so in that regard the movie delivers on its namesake. When it was being developed, the character model of Aki was conceived as being the world's first digital actress, with plans for her to appear in more movies after *The Spirits Within*, playing different roles.

Unfortunately, the film didn't even manage to break even at the box office, and so the newly formed Square Pictures was disbanded and merged back into Squaresoft (which is now known as Square Enix). It had a lukewarm critical reception, with some seeing it as visually stunning but not engaging on a narrative level.

Aki Ross (Ming-Na Wen) and the Deep Eyes Squad – © Colombia Pictures

Gray Edwards (Alec Baldwin) and Aki Ross (Ming-Na Wen) – © Colombia Pictures

WATCH IT FOR

The haunting sci-fi atmosphere, the revolutionary computer-generated characters and the vocal performances.

SEQUEL?

No sequel was produced, but, like the video game series, this was the norm apart from a few exceptions. *Final Fantasy X* was followed by *Final Fantasy X-2* and *Final Fantasy XIII* was followed by *Final Fantasy XIII-2* and *Lightning Returns: Final Fantasy XIII*. A collection of games followed *Final Fantasy VII*, and a number of titles such as *Final Fantasy XII* and *Final Fantasy Tactics* were set in the land of Ivalice.

This wasn't the last *Final Fantasy* movie to be produced, however. Arguably the most popular title in the series, *Final Fantasy VII*, received a CG movie sequel in 2005, called *Final Fantasy VII: Advent Children*. In it, Cloud and his companions had to deal with a mysterious plague-like disease and a trio of strangers who sought to resurrect the malicious being, Sephiroth. Likewise, the 2016 title *Final Fantasy XV* was given a movie in the form of *Kingsglaive: Final Fantasy XV*, whose events run concurrently with the game.

Final Fantasy VII: Advent Children – © Square Enix

Resident Evil

RELEASE DATE
12 July 2002

DIRECTOR
Paul W.S. Anderson

STARRING
Milla Jovovich,
Michelle
Rodriguez, James
Purefoy

TAGLINE
"SURVIVE THE
HORROR"

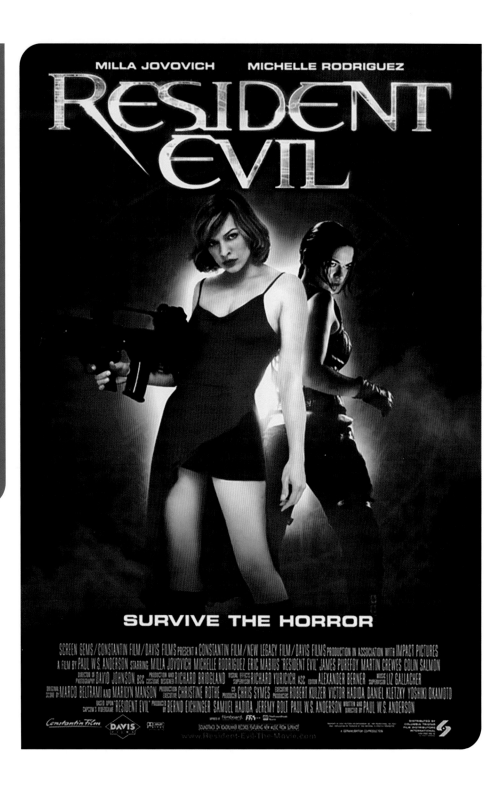

The *Resident Evil* series took the world by storm in 1996, bringing a nerve-shredding survival horror world to gamers on the PlayStation and continuing on to dozens of platforms after. The majority of the games follow the nefarious deeds of the Umbrella Corporation, a bio-weapons company posing as a leader in healthcare and pharmaceutical development. When one of their weapons, the T-virus, is unleashed in the American mid-western town of Raccoon City, residents are infected and turned into flesh-eating zombies and various other mutated abominations.

With a rotating cast of heroes including Chris and Claire Redfield, Leon S. Kennedy, Jill Valentine and Ethan Winters, the games have been incredibly successful for developer Capcom, spawning a multimedia franchise of spin-off games, novels and both CG and live-action movies. It is still wildly popular today, with the latest installment, *Resident Evil Village* (stylised as Resident Evil VII_I_AGE to indicate its position as the eighth main chapter) being released in May 2021 for the PlayStation 5, PlayStation 4, Xbox One, Xbox Series S & X and Windows.

> "You're ALL going to die down here..."
> – The Red Queen (Michaela Dicker)

The film rights to *Resident Evil* were acquired in 1998, and one of the earliest chosen directors was none other than the late zombie maestro George A. Romero, creator and director of the long-running 'of the Dead' series (*Night of the Living Dead, Dawn of the Dead, Day of the Dead, Land of the Dead, Diary of the Dead* & *Survival of the Dead*). Romero sought to base his film mostly on the original game, with Chris Redfield and Jill Valentine to star. However, after multiple scripts Romero's ideas were never approved, and he left the project. Despite this, it's said that some higher-ups at Capcom enjoyed his ideas.

Given the success of 1995's *Mortal Kombat*, Paul W.S. Anderson was chosen to write and direct, and he adapted a script he had written, titled *Undead* (which he admitted was heavily based on *Resident Evil*, after he had enjoyed playing the game), to shape it into a *Resident Evil* movie. The film released in 2002 and starred Milla Jovovich (*The Fifth Element, The Messenger: The Story of Joan of Arc, Monster Hunter*) as Alice, a woman who awakens in strange surroundings and with near-complete memory loss. After a military team takes her deep into an underground facility called the Hive, the group come across undead terrors and other creatures that have spawned as a result of mutations from the T-virus infection.

Resident Evil – © Capcom

Alice (Milla Jovovich) – © Sony Pictures Releasing

A 'licker' – © Sony Pictures Releasing

With an even mix of action and horror, Resident Evil isn't exactly similar to the games on which it's based. But it has a foreboding atmosphere, a sterile and eerie setting and pulse-pounding zombie action. The Cerberus dogs and a licker (both iconic enemies from the games) make their appearances along with a scene involving a booby-trapped corridor, which is a stand-out moment and sure to stick in viewers' minds for all the wrong reasons. The blood flows as the team try to finish their mission and escape the Hive intact. The movie was a massive success, and moderately received by critics.

WATCH IT FOR

The laser-protected corridor scene. It's arguably the most memorable scene in the whole movie series.

SEQUEL?

Yes. Only two years later, Alexander Witt directed *Resident Evil: Apocalypse*. The film continued to follow the journey of Alice, who was again played by Milla Jovovich.

Lara Croft: Tomb Raider – The Cradle of Life

RELEASE DATE
25 July 2003

DIRECTOR
Jan de Bont

STARRING
Angelina Jolie,
Gerard Butler,
Djimon Hounsou

Angelina Jolie returned two years later for *The Cradle of Life*, directed by action veteran Jan de Bont. The action-packed sequel sees Lara in search of the Cradle of Life, a mysterious and hidden location which supposedly houses Pandora's Box, an artifact of immense and terrible power. Unfortunately for the titular heroine, a bio-weapons expert and arms dealer called Jonathan Reiss (Ciarán Hinds – *The Terror, Game of Thrones*) is also on the hunt for the mythical location. The map to the cradle comes in the form of an orb, an object which Lara and her companions and Reiss' group of mercenaries both seek ruthlessly.

The action comes fast and thick in this sequel, and Jolie once again revels in her role. The comradery with Lara, Bryce and Hillary continues to be the heart of this series, and Ciarán Hinds is suitably cold and heartless as he sets out to bring a horrific plague down upon those he deems unworthy to live. Scottish actor Gerard Butler (*300, P.S. I Love You, Olympus Has Fallen*) co-stars as Terry Sheridan, an ex-lover of Lara's whose expertise she needs in order to locate the orb that can guide the way to the cradle.

From Greece to Shanghai to Tanzania, *The Cradle of Life* takes Lara all across the globe in what would turn out to be Jolie's final performance as the character. Featuring earthquakes, physics-defying caverns and thrilling freefalls, this movie feels like a kitchen sink approach to the action-adventure genre. Comedic moments are littered throughout, the majority of which come from Bryce and Hillary, their incredulity at their situation being the source of some genuine humour and heart. They play a more active role in Lara's adventure this time around, with their talents not just being delegated to housekeeping and ensuring Lara's plethora of gadgets are working at full capacity. This, along with some much more frightening peril than the first film, makes for a mesh of tones.

Weiss (Ciarán Hinds), Hillary (Chris Barrie), Bryce (Noah Taylor) and Lara (Angelina Jolie) – © Paramount Pictures

Lara (Angelina Jolie) and Terry (Gerard Butler) – © Paramount Pictures

A Shadow Guardian – © Paramount Pictures

The climax of the movie features some impressive set pieces and action-packed showdowns, along with questionable moral choices and of course, Lara caught in the middle. Similar to the 2001 film, the isolation of the games is lacking here, as Lara is almost constantly surrounded by friends or enemies. How much you enjoy it will be mostly based on your opinion of the first movie, as this is very much more of the same. It's a harmless action-adventure film that doesn't break any new ground, but then, it doesn't feel like it's trying to.

"Nature is about balance. All the world comes in pairs; Yin and Yang, right and wrong, men and women... What's pleasure without pain?

– Lara Croft (Angelina Jolie)

The film fared better critically than the original, but while a success, didn't make as much money as the 2001 film.

WATCH IT FOR

The scene towards the climax when Lara and the group are attacked by the ruthless Shadow Guardians. It's chilling and tense, and no one is safe.

SEQUEL?

No, although a third film was planned. Angelina Jolie declined to reprise her role as Lara Croft, as she felt she had achieved all that she wanted to within the franchise.

Following Crystal Dynamics' reboot of the video game series with 2013's *Tomb Raider*, a new film was developed. It was released in 2018 and starred Alicia Vikander in the lead role as Lara Croft.

House of the Dead

© Artisan Entertainment

RELEASE DATE
10 October 2003

DIRECTOR
Uwe Boll

STARRING
Jonathan Cherry, Ona Grauer, Clint Howard

TAGLINE
"You Won't Last the Night"

SEGA's light-gun series, *House of the Dead*, joined the ranks of classics like *Duck Hunt, Mad Dog McCree, Virtua Cop, Time Crisis* and *Point Blank* when it arrived in 1998. Now a bona fide arcade classic and staple of leisure centres around the world, this zombie-blasting action game has seen massive success, even on home consoles.

House of the Dead 2 gave the short-lived Dreamcast an arcade thrill-ride, and, using the Wii Zapper peripheral, players could lock and load their Wii remotes to annihilate the undead in *House of the Dead 2 & 3 Return* for Nintendo's massively successful console.

The Wii also saw the release of *House of the Dead: Overkill* (later ported to PS3), a gritty, grindhouse spin-off of the main series, filled with expletives, even more ridiculous gore and a '70s setting, complete with film grain and missing frames.

With five main entries (a remake of the original also saw release for Nintendo Switch) and a sixth on the way, *House of the Dead* has made a lasting impression on light-gun shooter fans. In

Left: *House of the Dead* – © SEGA

Below: The heroes of *House of the Dead* – © Artisan Entertainment

Rudy (Jonathan Cherry) – © Artisan Entertainment

2003, German director Uwe Boll was given the helm to a movie adaptation. This started what would be a long run of putting games to film for the controversial filmmaker.

Following a group of would-be ravers setting out to an island party, the movie wastes no time in setting the unwitting fodder up for their gruesome fates. When they arrive, the party has been abandoned, and it seems as though a fight of some sort has broken out. As they explore it becomes clear something altogether evil is occurring on this island paradise, and the undead quickly make their presence known.

"Shoot it!!"

– Greg (Will Sanderson)

"What do you think I am trying to do you f%*king moron?"

– Victor Kirk (Jürgen Prochnow)

When *House of the Dead* was released, Uwe Boll and his work would become a talking point for gamers around the world. The movie revels in its B-movie stylings, with over-the-top gore, stereotypically hormone-controlled couples who await their doom, and an absolutely bizarre performance by Clint Howard as Salish, first mate to Captain Kirk, who repeatedly tries to warn the young adults about the ominously named 'Isla de Morte' and the dangers they might face there.

The movie is intercut with scenes of gameplay directly from the video games and, while this might seem a bit on the nose, it really does help you realise how much of the tone of the series is kept intact. Filled with practical gore, Matrix-style 'bullet time' and a story that acts as a sort-of prequel to the original game, *House of the Dead* is a memorable film, no matter what you think of it.

It was poorly received by critics, but it started the long-running relationship between video game movies and the incomparable Uwe Boll.

WATCH IT FOR

The epic zombie kills, the dialogue and the song *Fury*, which plays over an extended bullet-time-filled massacre of the undead towards the final act of the film.

SEQUEL?

Yes. The movie was followed by the TV movie sequel, *House of the Dead II* (subtitled as *Dead Aim* in some releases), which featured a different cast and director (Michael Hurst). The screenwriter of the original movie, Mark A. Altman, also penned the script for this sequel. It dealt with questionable tests conducted by a scientist on a high school campus, which leads to a new outbreak of the undead. It was released in 2005, to a slightly better reception than the original.

Resident Evil: Apocalypse

RELEASE DATE
10 September 2004

DIRECTOR
Alexander Witt

STARRING
Milla Jovovich, Oded Fehr, Sienna Guillory

TAGLINE
"My Name is Alice, and I Remember Everything"

For the second installment in this massively successful series, director Alexander Witt came on board while Paul W.S. Anderson remained in a screenwriter capacity.

Taking place immediately after the events of the first film, Alice finds herself on her own, but determined, in a desolate, post-outbreak Raccoon City. As she searches for answers to the horrors she endured in the Hive, Alice comes across other survivors, chiefly Jill Valentine (Sienna Guillory – *Eragon*, *The Principles of Lust*) and Carlos Olivera (Oded Fehr – *The Mummy* & *The Mummy Returns*) whom gamers will know as the lead characters in *Resident Evil 3: Nemesis* and its 2020 remake, simply titled *Resident Evil 3*.

Nemesis, the hulking abomination that ruthlessly hunted players in 1999, makes his appearance here, having been hinted at during the previous movie's climax. There's a tinge of sadness surrounding his origins, showing the true tragedy of the viral outbreak and Umbrella's nefarious testing and disregard for human life. The survivors are contacted by Dr. Charles Ashford and are offered safe evacuation from the doomed city in exchange for finding his lost daughter, Angie.

Left: *Resident Evil 3: Nemesis* – © Capcom

Below: Nemesis – © Sony Pictures Releasing

Alice (Milla Jovovich), Angela Ashford (Sophie Vavasseur) and Jill Valentine (Sienna Guillory) – © Sony Pictures Releasing

The film, having escaped the confines of the claustrophobic Hive, features less foreboding tension and more action, with hordes of the undead littering the city. Along with the deadly Nemesis, the lickers return for a tense showdown in a church, and the terrifying Cerberus dogs attack when the group enter an elementary school in search of the missing girl.

"S.T.A.R.S!"

– Nemesis (Matthew G. Taylor)

Stylish and fast-paced, the movie strayed further from the source material and was mostly poorly received by critics, but it was a bigger box office success than the original film.

WATCH IT FOR

Nemesis. The Umbrella programmed monstrosity is honestly well recreated in this film, and his appearances are filled with genuine tension.

SEQUEL?

Absolutely. The movie was followed in 2007 by *Resident Evil: Extinction*, which saw *Highlander* director Russell Mulcahy take the helm, with Jovovich starring and Anderson once again penning the script.

Alone in the Dark

RELEASE DATE
28 January 2005

DIRECTOR
Uwe Boll

STARRING
Christian Slater,
Tara Reid,
Stephen Dorff

TAGLINE
"Evil Awakens"

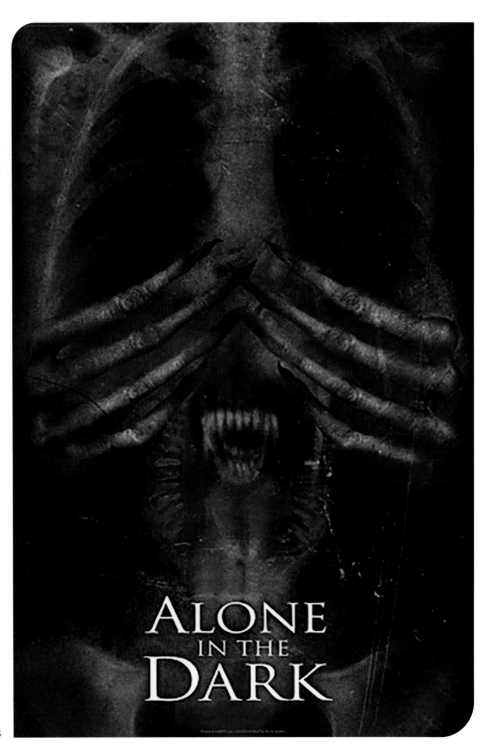

ALONE
IN THE
DARK

Alone in the Dark is the infamous adaptation of the classic survival-horror series. After House of the Dead, German director Uwe Boll and his crew were given the rights to a movie version of the gaming series that birthed an entire genre. While Resident Evil truly brought survival horror to the mainstream in 1996, it was Infogrames' DOS classic, Alone in the Dark, that created the atmospheric, dread-filled terror that gamers continue to enjoy to this day.

The original game, and to a lesser extent the first two sequels, are steeped in a Lovecraftian fear that makes them foreboding and fascinating. They gripped gamers and brought true, cinematic horror to legions of players who were just getting to grips with 3D gameplay. The hand-drawn backgrounds, minimalistic soundtrack and haunting setting – the massive mansion, Derceto – created an adventure like no other. It still has a rabid fanbase and the franchise continued with the reboot Alone in the Dark: The New Nightmare (2001 – PS1, PC, Dreamcast, Game Boy Color), a fifth game, Alone in the Dark (Xbox 360, Wii, PC, PS3 as Alone in the Dark: Inferno), which brought back the narrative from the original trilogy and, most recently, a co-operative multiplayer installment called Alone in the Dark: Illumination (2015 – PC).

Five of these six games starred Edward Carnby (Illumination starred Ted Carnby, a descendant of Edward), and so it was this iconic hero that made his way to the big screen, played by Christian Slater (True Romance, The Name of the Rose). Taking most of its narrative beats and characters from the standalone adventure, The New Nightmare, the movie deals with an ancient race called the Abkani, who opened portals to another world and meddled with the demons found on the other side.

Edward Carnby, one of many orphaned children with special powers, lives out his days as a paranormal private investigator. When he becomes a target for an artifact he possesses, he turns to his ex-girlfriend Aline Cedrac (Tara Reid – American Pie, The Big Lebowski) for help on how to decipher it and learn of its powers. Along the way he encounters Bureau 713, a group whom he used to be a part of, who are also tracing Abkani artifacts and the disturbances associated with them. Stephen Dorff (Blade, Leatherface) stars as Burke, an agent for the Bureau who has a storied history with Carnby. They reluctantly combine forces to trace a man who is trying to open a portal and let the demons beyond gain entrance to our world.

> "I think there's a vampire living in my closet, but my mommy says vampires and ghosts aren't real. She says there's nothing to be afraid of in the dark."
>
> – Boy

> "Your mother's wrong, kid. Being afraid of the dark is what keeps most of us alive."
>
> – Edward Carnby (Christian Slater)

Alone in the Dark – © THQ Nordic

Aline Cedrac (Tara Reid), Edward Carnby (Christian Slater) and Richard Burke (Stephen Dorff) – © Lions Gate Films

Alone in the Dark: The New Nightmare – © THQ Nordic

Alone in the Dark is known for being one of the worst movies ever made, going by its critical reception. It forgoes its title and the games it's based on by having a minimal amount of characters who are alone, and the tiniest fraction of scenes set in the dark. Like the *Resident Evil* movie series, AITD focuses more on action, with the soldiers of the Bureau and Edward Carnby taking on the creatures of darkness with flashlights, machine guns and a copious amount of strobe lights. It's another B-movie style offering from Uwe Boll, with a breakneck pace and editing, some *Matrix*-style bullet-time, and very loose links to the video games. It could be seen as a quasi-sequel to *The New Nightmare*, where Carnby and Aline Cedrac worked together on Shadow Island to defeat similar creatures and discover the fate of Carnby's old friend, Charles Fiske.

The last act of the movie does take place in a reasonably dark, labyrinthine cave system, similar to the ending of the original game and its sequel, *Alone in the Dark 2*, but the voodoo and Lovecraftian style of horror and dread from the video games is missing from this movie adaptation.

Despite its critical reception, it has remained a fascinating relic for games fans due to its infamous lack of cohesion and quality.

WATCH IT FOR

The most hilarious and inappropriate use of the song *7 Seconds* by Youssou N'Dour and Neneh Cherry.

SEQUEL?

Yes. Despite the critical and commercial failure of the film, a straight-to-video sequel, *Alone in the Dark 2*, was released in 2008. It was co-directed by the original movie's screenwriters, Peter Scheerer and Michael Roesch. Rick Yune replaced Christian Slater as Edward Carnby and horror and B-movie legend Lance Henriksen (*Aliens, Pumpkinhead*) starred in a supporting role. The movie bears little relation to the first and instead finds Carnby and a group of witch-hunters trying to track down an evil woman called Elizabeth Dexter. Like the original movie, it was not well received.

Doom

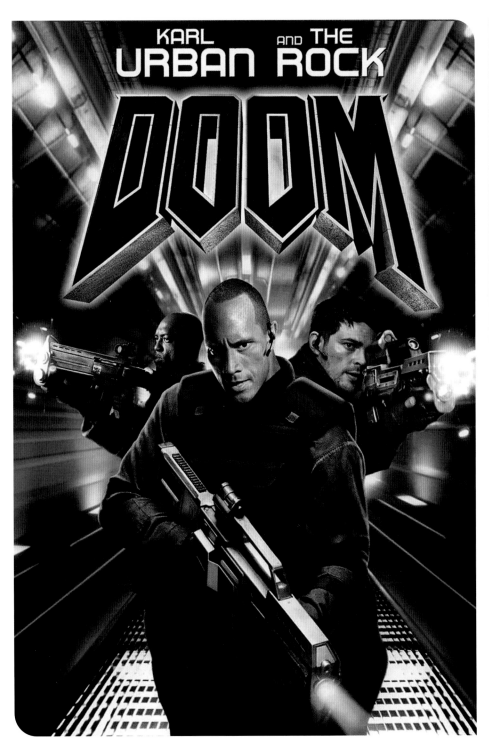

KARL URBAN AND THE ROCK

DOOM

RELEASE DATE
21 October 2005

DIRECTOR
Andrzej Bartkowiak

STARRING
Dwayne Johnson,
Karl Urban,
Rosamund Pike

TAGLINE
"Hell Breaks Loose"

Following in the footsteps of the trailblazing first-person shooter *Wolfenstein 3D, DOOM* garnered attention from gamers and critics alike for its atmospheric and frantic brand of shooting action. Tasking players with destroying a myriad of demons who have come through a portal from hell, it was revolutionary in its graphical and sound design. Despite being released after *Wolfenstein, DOOM*'s hellscapes stuck more in player's minds and went on to spawn a massive franchise that contained the original games and their mods and extra levels (*Final DOOM*) on PC, and also saw releases on the Nintendo 64 (*DOOM 64*) and Game Boy Advance. A 2016 reimagining, simply called *DOOM*, was released to massive critical acclaim, and a sequel, *DOOM Eternal*, followed in 2020. The first four games were released in 2019 for modern consoles (*DOOM, DOOM 2, DOOM 64* and *DOOM 3* - PS4, Xbox One, Nintendo Switch).

Shortly after the original release of the slower paced, atmospheric *DOOM 3* in 2004, the film adaptation began production, seeking to loosely adapt this release. Taking many cues in its design and story beats from James Cameron's classic sci-fi horror *Aliens* (1986), it stars former WWE wrestler Dwayne 'The Rock' Johnson (*The Scorpion King, Rampage, Moana*) as 'Sarge'. He's the leader of a military team sent through a portal to Mars to investigate a distress signal that was sent through to Earth. His team of ragtag soldiers includes John Grimm (Karl Urban – *The Lord of the Rings Trilogy, Dredd, The Boys*), a soldier with a connection to Samantha (Rosamund Pike – *Die Another Day, The Libertine, Pride & Prejudice*), one of the scientists on the Mars station.

The movie alters the origins of the demons significantly, but seeks to remain as dark and atmospheric as *DOOM 3*. Flickering lights, hidden silhouettes and ominous growls abound as the soldiers explore the aftermath of the carnage and seek to control and eliminate the spread of the hellish monsters. Naturally, not all of them survive, and the mystery surrounding the monsters' origins deepens as Samantha conducts autopsies, leading to some practical, gross-out moments.

> "I need soldiers! I don't need anyone else, but soldiers!"
>
> – Sarge (Dwayne Johnson)

The chemistry between The Rock and Karl Urban is a highlight of the film, and their evolving professional relationship is at the heart of the movie's drama. The Rock really seems like he's enjoying himself here, and, like his role in *Dredd*, Karl Urban is perfect as the grizzled soldier, Grimm, whose past is steeped in sadness.

Towards the climax of the movie there is a notable sequence filmed entirely in first-person. Recreating the feel of the game series, the scene is a treat for games fans, and genuinely feels like you're on some sort of ride as you watch it. Packing in the gore and demons, it's a love letter to the game series that spawned it.

DOOM – © Bethesda

Sarge (Dwayne Johnson), Grimm (Karl Urban) and the Marines – © Universal Pictures

DOOM 3 – © Bethesda

"It's this place, it's hell! It always was!"

– John Grimm (Karl Urban)

Despite its best efforts, *DOOM* was not a success at the box office and was negatively received by critics.

A hellish demon – © Universal Pictures

WATCH IT FOR

The first-person sequence. It's the closest thing to playing the game you're ever likely to see on film.

SEQUEL?

No sequel materialised for this flick, but a direct-to-video reboot called *DOOM: Annihilation* was released in 2019. It was written and directed by Tony Giglio and retained more of the traditional *DOOM* storyline than the 2005 film. It still didn't fare well with critics, although it was seen as a vast improvement over the previous movie.

BloodRayne

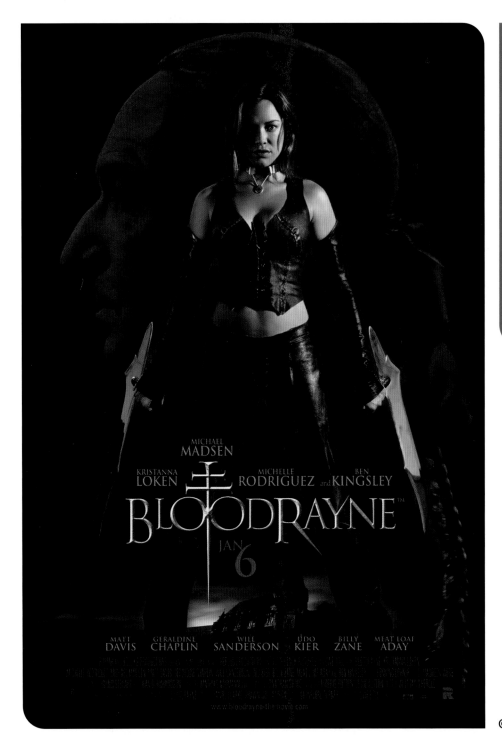

RELEASE DATE
6 January 2006

DIRECTOR
Uwe Boll

STARRING
Kristanna Loken,
Michael Madsen,
Ben Kingsley

Gothic action-adventure games saw much success in the PS1 and PS2 eras, with such franchises as *Nightmare Creatures* and the *Legacy of Kain* series satiating players' need for period-piece horror. The *BloodRayne* series (consisting of two fully 3D installments and a side-scrolling, downloadable release) continued this trend and follows human-vampire hybrid (or dhampir) Rayne, as she journeys throughout various time periods and occasionally completes missions for The Brimstone Society, a group that seeks to stop vampiric and other monstrous threats. The games are third-person hack-and-slash adventures, which allow players to use Rayne's various dhampir abilities, suck the blood of her enemies and use deadly weaponry in her various quests, which include infiltrating Nazi fortresses, defeating twisted cults and traversing ominous castles.

Director Uwe Boll, having brought *House of the Dead* and *Alone in the Dark* to the big screen, tried his hand at another horror-action video game franchise when the movie adaptation of *BloodRayne* was released in 2006. With Kristanna Loken (*Terminator 3: Rise of the Machines*, *In the Name of the King*) in the title role, it was Boll's most star-studded cast to date. Oscar winner Ben Kingsley (*Gandhi, Schindler's List, Shutter Island*) plays Rayne's father and the antagonist, while Michael Madsen, Michelle Rodriguez, Billy Zane and even rock music sensation Meat Loaf all appear in supporting roles.

Loosely adapting the series, it sees Rayne reluctantly join the Brimstone Society as she seeks vengeance on her tyrannical and unfeeling father Kagan (Kingsley) for the murder of her mother. Initially fearing Rayne's unholy curse, the members soon begin to realise that they have a common goal in the ending of Kagan's cruel plan of eliminating the human race.

To do that, they set out on a quest to find three artifacts: body parts of an ancient vampire called Belial, who found ways to overcome the weaknesses inherent in vampires. Knowing Kagan's need for these abilities, Rayne and her companions race against time and foe alike to gather these powers before the powerful vampire lord.

"I would never have believed it could have been so EASY."

– Kagan (Ben Kingsley)

Filled with torch-lit chambers, buckets of blood and miles-long exposition, *BloodRayne* keeps a similar tone to Boll's previous adaptations. Kristanna Loken is not dissimilar to her previous character, the Terminatrix, as she slashes and bites through a variety of enemies throughout the

BloodRayne – © Terminal Reality

Rayne (Kristanna Loken) – © Boll KG Productions

**Kagan (Ben Kingsley) – ©
Boll KG Productions**

movie. Ben Kingsley is content to sit on his throne for the majority of the film, sending grand, sweeping proclamations and threats intermittently until Rayne arrives for the final showdown. Michelle Rodriguez throws out her best British accent in keeping with the eighteenth century setting, a far cry from her role as Letty Ortiz in the *Fast & Furious* series. Meat Loaf hams it up as only he can as vampire lord Leonid, as he lies in a luxurious bed surrounded by naked women. The women in question were played by real-life Romanian prostitutes, as Uwe Boll noted they were cheaper to hire than extras.

For any fans of Boll's previous game-to-film works, this movie is sure to entertain on some level. For hardcore fans of the video game, it's probably a different story.

BloodRayne was poorly received by critics and only grossed $4 million of its $25 million budget.

WATCH IT FOR

Ben Kingsley's bizarrely distant performance, Michelle Rodriguez's British accent and Rayne's fight with a giant, deformed monk.

SEQUEL?

Yes, Uwe Boll returned to the director's chair for not one, but two direct-to-video sequels. *BloodRayne 2: Deliverance* (2007) and *BloodRayne: The Third Reich* (2011) instead starred Natassia Malthe, and saw Rayne do battle with Billy the Kid in the wild west and Nazis during the Second World War. Like the original, both movies were poorly received.

Silent Hill

RELEASE DATE
21 April 2006

DIRECTOR
Christophe Gans

STARRING
Radha Mitchell,
Sean Bean,
Deborah Kara
Unger

TAGLINE
"We've Been
Expecting You"

Horror-themed games seemed to be intriguing for Hollywood during the 2000s. Following on from other survival horror staples like *Resident Evil* and *Alone in the Dark, Silent Hill* was adapted by director Christophe Gans in 2006. The game series was known for its unique brand of psychological horror, which developer Konami brought to the PlayStation for the first time in 1999.

The original game saw Harry Mason searching the fictional town of *Silent Hill* for his missing daughter, Cheryl. As he explores the ghost town, Harry comes across and does battle with a host of hideous and twisted creatures, as the town itself seems to shift between the abandoned mid-western locale and a horrifying, metallic hellscape. The series was a massive success, and many sequels followed, each containing a new protagonist but keeping the same brand of unpredictable terror. The series was set to be rebooted under the supervision of *Metal Gear Solid* creative director Hideo Kojima, with Norman Reedus (*The Walking Dead, The Boondock Saints, Ride*) to lend his voice and likeness to the game. *Silent Hills* never materialised, and the only remains are the demo known as *P.T. (Playable Teaser)*.

Gans sought to recreate that terror on screen, and so the movie loosely adapts the storyline of the first game. Radha Mitchell stars as Rose Da Silva, who takes her daughter Sharon on a drive to find the town of Silent Hill, a name which Sharon continually mentions during

Silent Hill – © Konami

Rose Da Silva (Radha Mitchell) – © TriStar Pictures

dangerous bouts of sleepwalking. On the way, their car is forced off the road as Rose attempts to avoid a human shape in their path. When she awakens, she finds Sharon missing, and sets off on foot into the town of Silent Hill to find her.

The movie is notable for keeping many elements of the game intact. Some of the creatures bear massive resemblances to their game counterparts, and one of the initial scenes involving Rose discovering a crucified and disembowelled body before being chased by pint-sized intruders is lifted straight from the original game, and is terrifyingly realised on film. Series staple Pyramid Head – a large, hulking demon from the other world – makes his presence known, and hunts the characters ruthlessly when he appears. The familiar faceless nurses steal a scene in the later part of the movie, and video game characters such as the police officer Cybil and the mysterious, cloaked lady Dahlia Gillespie are present and accounted for.

> "Only the Dark One opens and closes the door to Silent Hill…"
> – Dahlia Gillespie (Deborah Kara Unger)

Played concurrently with Rose's trip through hell is her husband's attempts to locate his missing wife and daughter. Christopher Da Silva (Sean Bean – *Game of Thrones, The Lord of the Rings Trilogy, Goldeneye*) traverses the real world, working with police and occasionally bending the law to find any information on the town of Silent Hill and clues to the whereabouts of his family.

The video games have iconic soundtracks composed by Akira Yamaoka, and in keeping with the idea of recreating the experience of the games, composer Jeff Danna ensured that the entire movie soundtrack consisted of Yamaoka's themes. Some of these are rearranged and some are exactly as they appeared in the game versions. This authenticity is at the heart of the movie adaptation of *Silent Hill*, which arguably goes further than the majority of video game films in its attempt to celebrate the source material and please long-time fans.

The disfigured nurses hunt Rose – © TriStar Pictures

Silent Hill received mostly negative reviews from critics, although its visuals were praised. It was also a box office success, grossing two times its budget.

WATCH IT FOR

The unsettling atmosphere, the faithful recreations of moments and creatures from the games, and the hauntingly beautiful soundtrack.

SEQUEL?

Yes. *Silent Hill: Revelation* was released in 2012 and was directed by Michael J. Bassett. Radha Mitchell, Sean Bean and Deborah Kara Unger (Dahlia Gillespie) all reprised their roles.

DOA: Dead or Alive

© Dimension Films

Tecmo's *Dead or Alive* franchise generated massive buzz, but not only for its brand of bone-crunching one-on-one fighting. The female fighters play a huge role in the series, even generating their own spin-off games, *Dead or Alive Xtreme* – which originally featured volleyball but has since expanded to include even more sports and minigames. When *Dead or Alive 2* was released in arcades in 1999 and then on PlayStation 2 and Dreamcast in 2000, it gained huge notoriety for the design of its female characters.

While the 1996 original was still a little provocative, the sequel saw the introduction of a new graphics engine, and a new focus on the anatomy of the female fighters. With a specific focus on the physics of their breasts, *Dead or Alive* gained fans and detractors for its depiction of these characters. Nevertheless, the game series is a massive success and a legitimately hardcore and intricate addition to the fighting game space. The most recent entry, *Dead or Alive 6*, was released in arcades and on PC, Xbox One and PlayStation 4 in 2019.

While the character of Kasumi has long been the heroine of the franchise, for the movie version of *Dead or Alive* the filmmakers chose to focus on a trio of characters, and much of

Dead or Alive –
© Tecmo

the plot and marketing is built around them. Devon Aoki plays Kasumi, an exiled shinobi who accepts an invitation to the *Dead or Alive* tournament solely to look for her missing brother Hayate, who was involved in the previous tournament. Holly Valance plays Christie, a professional thief who accepts her spot in the tournament for a chance to steal the cash prize and anything else she can find. Finally, Jaime Pressly plays the professional wrestler Tina, who accepts a place in order to prove that she can win a fight beyond the ring. Joining them are a whole cast of characters from the game series, including but not limited to: the hero of the *Ninja Gaiden* reboot series Hayabusa, Tina's wrestler father Bass, the mowhawk sporting ladies-man Zack, and Ayane, an assassin seeking to kill Kasumi and eliminate her shame from their group (Ayane is played by Natassia Malthe, who played Rayne in the two *BloodRayne* sequels).

The movie, like many adaptations, is fast-paced, and before the tournament even begins, martial arts abound. From Kasumi's escape to Christie's barely-clothed battle to Tina's fight on open water, the movie wastes no time in bringing the action to viewers. Robin Shou, who played Liu Kang in 1995's *Mortal Kombat* and its 1997 sequel, *Annihilation*, plays one of the goons who tries to attack Tina on her boat.

> "Look Little Miss Zen Master, this isn't Karate Kid, it's DOA. As in Dead or Alive. As in ten million dollars!"
>
> – Tina Armstrong (Jaime Pressly)

**Ayane (Natassia Malthe) – ©
Dimension Films**

Christie (Holly Valance) – © Dimension Films

Eric Roberts plays Victor Donovan, the man in charge of setting up the tournament, and his reasons for doing so are explored as the film goes on. He's the constant shadow hanging over proceedings, which includes an inventive family battle on some frail rafts, a ninja showdown in a bamboo thicket and an homage to the *Xtreme* games where the ladies of the *DOA* world play some recreational volleyball.

DOA: Dead or Alive doesn't pretend to be anything other than what it is: a campy, sexualised late-night movie that lets you zone out for the better part of two hours and enjoy some admittedly impressive martial arts against a tropical backdrop with scantily clad women and cheesy one-liners. Action director and choreographer Corey Yuen (*The Transporter*) does a great job of giving the fight scenes the right pace, and the deep, bassy crunch of action that the game series is known for.

DOA was poorly received by critics and failed at the box office.

WATCH IT FOR

The great choreography, the cheery island setting and the three deadly, showstopping heroines.

SEQUEL?

No. The lack of critical or commercial success meant no further adaptations of *Dead or Alive* came about. The game series however, continues to thrive.

Resident Evil: Extinction

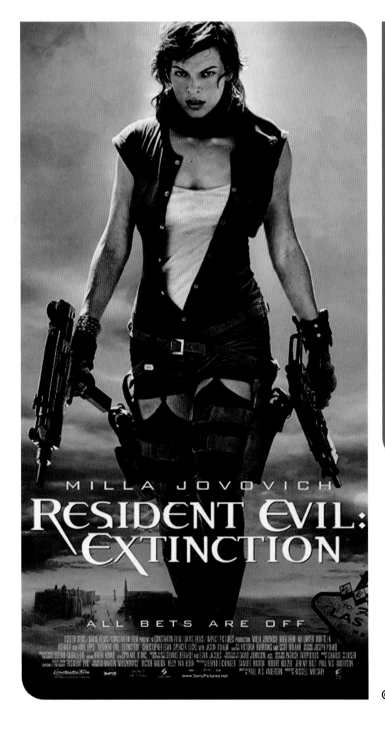

RELEASE DATE
21 September 2007

DIRECTOR
Russell Mulcahy

STARRING
Milla Jovovich, Oded Fehr, Ali Larter

TAGLINE
"All Bets Are Off"

© Sony Pictures Releasing

The third movie in the action-horror series saw Russell Mulcahy (*Highlander*) take the director's chair. Paul W.S. Anderson wrote the screenplay once again, bringing the action to the Nevada desert this time around.

Following on from the events of *Apocalypse*, the movie sees Alice on her continuing mission to end the outbreak instigated by the evil Umbrella Corporation. She re-teams with some of the survivors of the previous movie and iconic series heroine, Claire Redfield, played by Ali Larter. Together, the group of survivors traverse the deserts in search of supplies and a new hope that can turn the tide against the deadly outbreak that has now ravaged the majority of the world.

Pulling the strings for the deplorable Umbrella corporation is main series villain Albert Wesker, whose confidence and ruthlessness make him a formidable leader for the nefarious work going on behind the scenes. As Wesker delivers commands to other high-ranking members of Umbrella, such as Iain Glen's Dr. Isaacs, Alice and her companions must survive the harsh wild of the Nevada desert, which is rife with undead activity. Swarms of zombies relentlessly hunt the heroes for their flesh, while infected crows (a video game series classic) confront the survivors in a brutal, hectic and ultimately fatal stand-off.

Alice is no stranger to watching those around her become victims to the horrendous T-Virus, but this time around she must contend with a horrifying reality about her origins. This drives her however, and her quest for revenge takes on a whole new level of rage and determination. Her fury culminates in a battle with a Tyrant, a disfigured and mutated beast which was reserved for final boss status in the early games in the series.

Once again, the movie series of *Resident Evil* has its foot placed firmly in action territory, with slow horror moments drizzled in between. If comparisons could be drawn, they would mostly be to *Resident Evil 5* (2009), despite being released two years later, which saw Chris Redfield and Sheva Alomar attempt to destroy the "Las Plagas" infection in a fictional African country. The sun-kissed towns are the closest comparison in the games to the Nevada desert setting in Extinction, but ultimately, it's not really worth comparing beyond that. With *Extinction*, Paul Anderson truly began to branch his movie series off in a whole different direction from the game series it's based on.

The movie was a box office success like its predecessors, but had a mostly negative critical reception. Its action was the source of some positive reviews.

Resident Evil 5 –
© **Capcom**

Above: Claire Redfield (Ali Larter) and Alice (Milla Jovovich) – © Sony Pictures Releasing

Right: The infected birds attack – © Sony Pictures Releasing

"You won't have to wait that long boys. Because I'm coming for you, and I'm gonna be bringing a few of my friends..."

– Alice (Milla Jovovich)

WATCH IT FOR

The scene in which infected crows attack the group of survivors. It's genuinely pulse-pounding and bleak for the heroes.

SEQUEL?

Yes, another installment of zombie-slaying action was released in 2010, called *Resident Evil: Afterlife*. Paul W.S. Anderson wrote the film and, for the first time since the 2002 original, he returned as director. The film once again starred his real-life wife (the couple met on the set of the 2002 movie, and wed in 2009) Milla Jovovich, as the super-human heroine, Alice.

Postal

RELEASE DATE
18 October 2007

DIRECTOR
Uwe Boll

STARRING
Zach Ward,
Dave Foley,
J.K. Simmons

TAGLINE
"Disgusting.
Offensive.
Stupid."

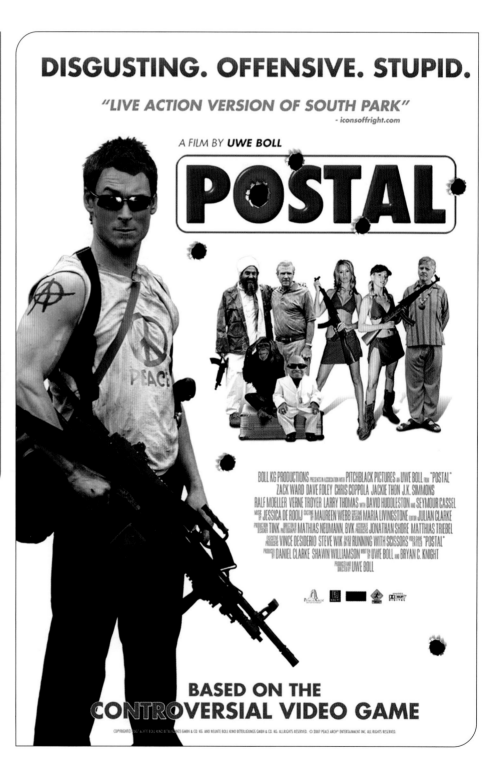

*P*ostal is by far the least politically correct video game adaptation to come to the silver screen. Under the direction of Uwe Boll, the ludicrous antics that occur in Paradise, Arizona, manage to rip every race, religion and sexual identity to shreds in an hour and forty minutes.

The *Postal* video game series has evolved since developer Running with Scissors released the original in 1997. An isometric shooter, the game saw a man go 'postal' and begin a crazed spree of violence after believing his town was being polluted with noxious gas. It notably featured hyper-violent shootouts and a dark, bizarre story which was well received by critics and spawned several sequels.

Postal 2 (the main basis for the movie adaptation) arrived in 2003 and significantly changed the style of gameplay. While it still contained, and heightened, the offbeat humour and gratuitous violence, the game was a first-person shooter. *Postal III* followed in 2011, to poor critical and fan reception, and even the developers have shown regret at how the final product turned out. The most recent entry, *Postal 4: No Regerts* (not a typo!), was released in Early Access (a sort of BETA phased rollout that allows players to give the developers feedback before the final product is released) in 2019.

Uwe Boll acquired the rights to the series after the release of *Postal 2* and worked on the script with Bryan C. Knight. The movie stars Zach Ward (*Resident Evil: Apocalypse, Alone in the Dark II*) as the 'postal dude', a down on his luck everyman who lives in the ironically named

Postal 2 – © **Running With Scissors**

The Postal Dude (Zach Ward) – © Boll KG Productions

'Paradise' in Arizona. While the dude is searching for a job as his wife cheats on him with numerous town residents, his uncle, Dave (played by Dave Foley, comedian and founding member of Canadian troupe *The Kids in the Hall*), brings him a proposition which he believes will make them both rich. Dave wants his nephew to help him steal a shipment of much sought-after 'Krotchy' dolls. The humanoid- testicle character is lifted straight from *Postal 2* and in the movie and game has become a sensation across the world.

What follows is a cacophony of blood, racist insults and sex as Dave and the postal dude come to multiple stand-offs with none other than Osama Bin Laden and the Al'Qaeda, who want to claim the Krotchy dolls for themselves. There's no way of getting around it; *Postal* will probably offend you or gross you out in some fashion throughout its run time. If starting the movie with the 9/11 attacks doesn't sound like your cup of tea, stay right away. If it does, expect copious amounts of violence, swearing in every other sentence, full-frontal nudity, and the concept of Verne Troyer (playing himself) getting defiled by monkeys.

In a notable scene at a German festival, director Uwe Boll appears as himself, giving a mock interview about his video game adaptations and how they're financed. Boll gets into a fight on screen with *Postal* creator Vince Desi in one of the movie's most memorable moments, before absolute carnage breaks out at the festival.

"I hate video games..."

– Uwe Boll as himself

Postal is a movie that definitely retains the mood of its source material, showcasing the most politically incorrect jokes it can, tons of violent escapades and a ludicrous storyline that has Osama Bin Laden and George W. Bush portrayed as best friends. Its humour might fall flat for some, but conversely, many will be able to go along for the ride and have a good time.

It all depends on your tolerance for low-brow comedy. Actors like Zach Ward and Dave Foley are engaging and genuinely funny with the material they're given, and Verne Troyer definitely has no problem poking fun at himself. The movie can't be faulted for its enthusiasm.

**Osama Bin Laden and George W. Bush... besties –
© Boll KG Productions**

Uwe Boll would appear as a non-player character in *Postal III*, the next installment released after the movie.

Postal was not well received by critics and only grossed 1% of its budget.

WATCH IT FOR

Late-night entertainment, the performances of Zach Ward and Dave Foley, and the fight between the director and the creator of the video game series. Just make sure whoever you're watching with knows what they're getting themselves in for!

SEQUEL?

There were plans for a sequel to the controversial comedy, with Uwe Boll returning to direct. A Kickstarter page was opened on 28 August 2013 with a view to funding another installment. The $500,000 goal was never met however, and the project was cancelled.

Hitman

RELEASE DATE
30 November
2007

DIRECTOR
Xavier Gens

STARRING
Timothy
Olyphant,
Dougray Scott,
Olga Kurylenko

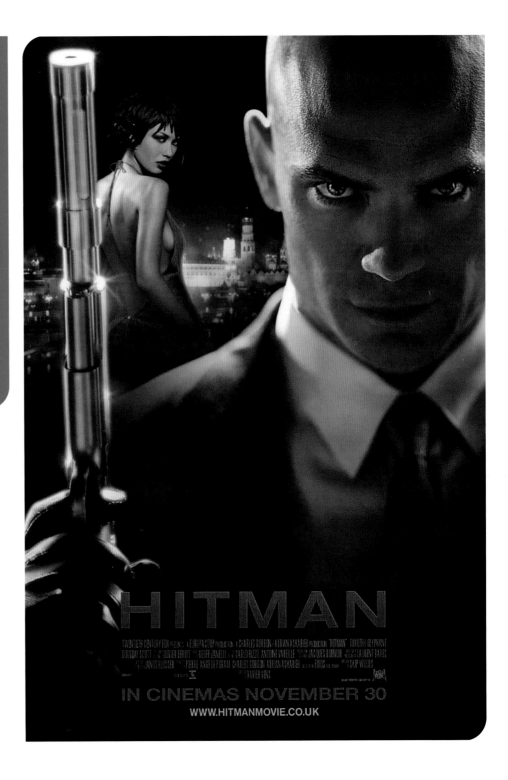

As of 2021, the *Hitman* series sits at eight releases, each following Agent 47, a trained assassin who takes on contracts from a variety of agencies and removes his targets with stealth and deadly accuracy. The game series is notable for its open-ended approach to missions, as players are given a target, a multitude of weapons and set loose in a sandbox location to attempt to assassinate their prey. It proved a huge success with gamers around the world for its innovation in player choice and the reactions of non-player characters to the decisions of the player.

The success of the games – which had four installments prior to the film's release – made it a prime candidate for the big screen. Although Vin Diesel was originally in talks to play Agent 47, he eventually had to turn it down, and Timothy Olyphant (*Justified, Santa Clarita Diet, The Mandalorian*) took up the lead role. Loosely adapting the video games, the film sees Agent 47 taking on a number of hits for a shadowy group known only as 'The Organization'. Like the games, he does this in stealthy and hyper-violent ways, picking off his targets unseen and leaving the scene soon after.

After a standard, but explosive, hit, Agent 47 quickly finds himself drawn into a Russian conspiracy, and he goes on the run to escape as he now finds himself the target of a number of assassination attempts. Along with Nika (Olga Kurylenko), Agent 47 attempts to uncover the truth regarding the set-up, all while being chased by Interpol member Mike Whittier (Dougray Scott).

Hitman visually captures the feeling of the games, and Timothy Olyphant has just the right amount of personality in the role, which calls for a distant, but wholly clever protagonist. Free from extreme emotions, it makes some of 47's actions both easier and tougher to

Right: Agent 47 in the original *Hitman: Codename 47* – © IO Interactive

Below: Agent 47 (Timothy Olyphant) – © 20th Century Fox

Nika Boronina (Olga Kurylenko) and Agent 47 (Timothy Olyphant) – © 20th Century Fox

stomach. There are genuinely thrilling assassinations to be found in the movie, perhaps not as elaborate as some of the levels in the game series, but seeing Agent 47 pose as a high-profile arms dealer to infiltrate a meeting feels like it came straight from the source.

> "I told you to leave her alone. You should have listened."
>
> – Agent 47 (Timothy Olyphant)

The tension is fairly high throughout, as the hitman is pursued on all fronts, from Interpol to the determined Russian officer Yuri Marklov (Robert Knepper – *Prison Break, Heroes, iZombie*), but the slower moments with Agent 47 and Nika help to give nuance to a character that has been trained to be completely unfeeling.

Some critics enjoyed *Hitman*, but it was mostly poorly received. It was, however, a massive success at the box office.

WATCH IT FOR

Some great assassinations, Timothy Olyphant's performance and the labyrinthine, globe-trotting plot.

SEQUEL?

No direct sequel to this version of *Hitman* came about, but the series was rebooted in 2015 as *Hitman: Agent 47*, with Rupert Friend now in the title role.

In the Name of the King: A Dungeon Siege Tale

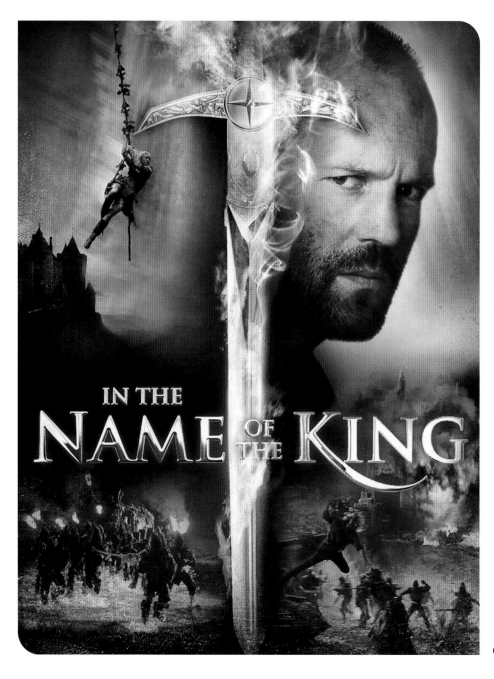

RELEASE DATE
11 January 2008

DIRECTOR
Uwe Boll

STARRING
Jason Statham,
Leelee Sobieski,
Ray Liotta

TAGLINE
"Rise and Fight"

Dungeon Siege –
© **Gas Powered**
Games

U we Boll once again returned to the video game field with this big-screen adaptation of the *Dungeon Siege* series of PC role-playing games, developed by Gas Powered Games. The dungeon-crawling RPGs take place in the kingdom of Ehb, and are notable for their hordes of enemies, non-stop action (atypical of most role-playing games at the time) and a seamless world which was a whole, rather than being broken up into various levels. It follows a farmer as he attempts to stop an invading force of monsters, gains a number of companions, and ultimately learns more of the wicked intentions of the Krug and their plans for the once peaceful kingdom.

Dungeon Siege (2002) proved to be a big success for Gas Powered Games, and critics were impressed at its ability to buck genre conventions and give players a fast-paced, relentless game world which kept action at its heart. It was followed by add-ons (as well as having a vibrant modding community which was encouraged by the developers) and sequels, *Dungeon Siege II* (2005) and *Dungeon Siege III* (2011).

The movie went into production after the release of *Dungeon Siege II*, and had a notably larger budget than any of Boll's previous video game movies. He once again managed to secure an all-star cast filled with industry veterans, such as Burt Reynolds, Ray Liotta, Leelee Sobieski and John Rhys-Davies. Looking to mirror the success of previous fantasy films such as Peter Jackson's *The Lord of the Rings* trilogy, the movie was graced with the lengthy title *In the Name of the King: A Dungeon Siege Tale* and released in 2008.

The film follows the quest of Farmer (Jason Statham – *The Transporter* series, *Hobbs & Shaw*) as he seeks vengeance for the wrong-doings of the wicked sorcerer Gallian (Ray Liotta – *Goodfellas*), who tries to rule the kingdom with the aid of his powerful magic and an army of obiedient and vicious monsters, the Krug. Adept with a sword and a boomerang, Farmer joins forces with members of the king's army in order to quell the Krug invasion and rid the Kingdom of Ehb of the threat of the powerful magician. Farmer's long-time friend Norick (Ron Perlman – *Hellboy, Alien Resurrection*) aids him in his journey, and the two work with a variety of

Farmer (Jason Statham), Muriella (Leelee Sobieski) and Commander Tarish (Brian J. White) – © 20th Century Fox

companions, most notably a noble magician named Merick (John Rhys-Davies – *The Lord of the Rings Trilogy, Raiders of the Lost Ark*) and a woodland nymph named Elora (Kristanna Loken – *Terminator 3: Rise of the Machines, BloodRayne*).

"You gonna fight? Or talk me to death?"

– Farmer (Jason Statham)

This release shouldn't surprise viewers who have seen any of Uwe Boll's previous movies based on video games. *In the Name of the King* has a very *Hercules: The Legendary Journeys* vibe about it, with the battles being mostly harmless and lacking any real impact. The Krug and the humans are sliced and kicked, but no real evidence of their wounds or realism to go with the actions on screen is to be found. Instead, characters elaborately fall and flip out of shot with the momentum, but not much blood or injuries follow. This detracts a little from the seriousness of the battles being waged, and gives the movie a strangely empty feeling when it comes to the combat.

Likewise, the dialogue is either wooden or delivered with completely over-the-top bombast; there is no in-between. Some of the exchanges between Statham and Perlman can bring about a smile, but the awkward inflections and choppy editing, coupled with the fact that Jason Statham is as he would be in any modern-day action movie setting, is hard to ignore. Matthew Lillard seems to be in his element as Fallow, the king's nephew who serves the evil mage, Gallian. Lillard can't be faulted for his enthusiasm, as he laughs and screams and worms his

Norick (Ron Perlman) and Solana (Claire Forlani) – © 20th Century Fox

way through the movie in a supporting role. Likewise, Ray Liotta is a comical villain more than a terrifying one, and Farmer easily dispatches the proxy warriors Gallian controls remotely, leaving little tension in his schemes.

In the Name of the King swings a lot closer to something like *Eragon* rather than the grand, sweeping spectacle of *The Lord of the Rings*. There is nothing inherently wrong with the film, but viewers should know what to expect when it comes to Boll's video game movies. Hammy dialogue, questionable editing and actors who are most certainly only present to pick up a pay check, this fantasy movie ticks all of the boxes associated with Uwe Boll's B-movie sensibilities.

It was Boll's first and last big-budget feature, as it failed to make back the majority of its costs and was not well received by critics.

WATCH IT FOR

Jason Statham and Ron Perlman's moments of genuine comradery, the occasional nifty fight scene and John Rhys-Davies being his usual excellent self as the magician, Merick.

SEQUEL?

Yes, despite the negative financial results, Uwe Boll returned for two sequels that went straight to home video. First came *In the Name of the King 2: Two Worlds* in 2011, which starred Dolph Lundgren as a modern-day soldier transported to the kingdom of Ehb, where he must battle an evil leader known as Raven. In 2014, Boll directed *In the Name of the King 3: The Last Mission*, with Dominic Purcell as an assassin who is likewise sent to Ehb to save the kingdom from the wicked Tervon. Both movies were poorly received.

Far Cry

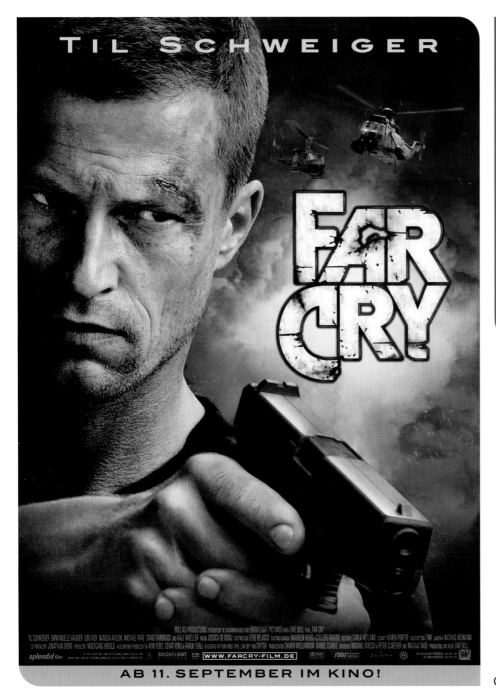

RELEASE DATE
2 October 2008

DIRECTOR
Uwe Boll

STARRING
Til Schweiger,
Emmanuelle
Vaugier, Udo Kier

Crytek sought to shake up the first-person shooter genre when it launched *Far Cry* in 2004. The game, which saw ex-soldier Jack Carver do battle with mercenaries on a tropical island, utilised Crytek's new CryEngine, which allowed for dynamic and realistic physics and unparalleled graphical fidelity. As a result, it was only initially available on PC, and it required a high-end machine at that.

Nevertheless, it was still successful, giving players multiple ways to approach and dispatch enemies and complete missions. After the first game, Crytek passed the rights to the series on to Ubisoft, who continued with spin-offs and five main sequels, most recently *Far Cry 6* in 2021. Crytek moved on to its popular and graphically intensive *Crysis* series, releasing three installments as well as remasters for modern consoles.

In 2008, one month before the release of *Far Cry 2* on PC and consoles, Uwe Boll directed a film adaptation of *Far Cry*. Loosely following the first game's story, Til Schweiger took the lead role as Jack Carver, accompanying Emmanuelle Vaugier's Valerie Cardinal to an island where she believed a scientist was conducting bizarre experiments on human subjects.

> "Absolutely outstanding..."
>
> – Dr. Krieger (Udo Kier)

Carver and Cardinal traverse the island to find out the truth, dealing with Dr. Krieger's henchmen and his super-human creations. This is, to date, Uwe Boll's final new video game

Far Cry – © Ubisoft

Jack Carver (Til Schweiger) and Dr. Krieger (Udo Kier) – © Boll KG Productions

movie property - but not his final adaptation, as seen by the BloodRayne and Dungeon Siege sequels - as the director went on to make more personal projects, such as the generally well-received *Rampage* series (not to be confused with the *Rampage* video game movie), which saw three movies, with a fourth on the way.

Unfortunately, instead of falling into so-bad-it's-good territory like Tommy Wiseau's *The Room* (2003) or some of Boll's other work, *Far Cry* commits the biggest crime possible for a movie: it's uneventful. The epic, tropical shoot-outs that made the first game so exhilarating are few and far between here, and there are a multitude of scenes, often in a row, that slow the film to a crawl. Some of these slower scenes even lack a score, which makes it feel empty and as though the actors are winging their performances while waiting for the scene to cut.

It's a shame, because *Far Cry* seems like a perfect vehicle for a movie adaptation. Each installment of the game is standalone, with different characters and locations, all keeping the same theme of a player character out of their depth in an open or semi-open world while contending with threatening villains. Granted, the only game in the series to have been released when production began was the original *Far Cry*, so Carver's adventure was the perfect choice on paper.

The bright colours and tropical locales of the game are muted on film, and while the movie technically looks crisp, the laboratory scenes take up much of the run time and so audiences are left with a lot of cold, grey sterility.

Til Schweiger does his best as Jack Carver, but he's not given a lot to work with. Emmanuelle Vaugier is perfectly fine in her supporting role, and the two do have brief moments of genuine chemistry and humour. Likewise, Cardinal has her share of action moments throughout her

Dr. Krieger (Udo Kier) and an enhanced soldier – © Boll KG Productions

investigation. Like any movie, especially an Uwe Boll work, *Far Cry* likely has some fans out there who either genuinely like it or ironically enjoy its cheesy dialogue, but it's a struggle to believe it would please fans of the games.

Far Cry was critically panned and didn't make a dent at the box office.

WATCH IT FOR

Til Schweiger's performance as Carver, and a boat chase scene in the final act of the movie.

SEQUEL?

No, Boll's *Far Cry* never saw a follow-up, but there have been rumours of a new version of a *Far Cry* movie ramping up recently.

Max Payne

RELEASE DATE
17 October 2008

DIRECTOR
John Moore

STARRING
Mark Wahlberg, Mila Kunis, Beau Bridges

Remedy Entertainment's *Max Payne* thrilled gamers with its unique brand of gritty, neo-noir shooting action when it was released in 2002. It follows the grizzled ex-police officer as he works his way through a criminal underworld after experiencing a crippling personal tragedy. With an inspired narrative told in a comic book style, well-written characters that ooze personality, and exciting shooting mechanics that are responsive and satisfying, it's no surprise that *Max Payne* and its two sequels are still remembered fondly by gamers today.

In 2008, the first game in the series was the source of a movie adaptation, directed by John Moore and placing Mark Wahlberg in the lead role. Similar to the game, Max Payne loses his wife and child in a tragic turn of events that set him on a desperate quest and into the depths of the city's criminal underworld. With his personal tragedy silently motivating him, the cold case detective, along with his video game companion Mona Sax (Mila Kunis – *Family Guy*, *Bad Moms*), stumbles upon a dangerous and insidious plan to create super-powered soldiers. Max and Mona link this plan to the city's rampant use of a dangerous drug that causes enhanced abilities to some, but horrific side-effects to others.

As the duo delve deeper and interrogate anyone they can find a lead to, Max begins to see links between this dangerous venture and the tragedy that befell his family. Mona aids Max in his investigation into the mysterious Aesir company. The result is a trippy, stylish movie that definitely pushes for style over substance.

Max Payne – © Rockstar Games

"I don't believe in heaven. I believe in pain. I believe in fear. I believe in death."
– Max Payne (Mark Wahlberg)

Taking some liberties with a franchise is to be expected, and *Max Payne* is no different. The circumstances surrounding Max's redemption are revealed at a different pace to the game, leaving viewers with more mystery surrounding the detective's motives. The movie itself blurs the lines between reality and fantasy, as the Valkyr drug causes intense hallucinations for those whose biology it can't quite meld to. Because of this, *Max Payne* has some bizarre, ethereal scenes that might be jarring for people who like their gritty action more grounded. That being said, Mark Wahlberg does a good job conveying Max as a broken, but determined man, and it's refreshing to see Mila Kunis, known mostly for her comedic turns, play the iconic Mona Sax. Not just present as a sidekick, Mona has her own reasons for getting embroiled in the seedy machinations of the New York underworld.

Max Payne is comparable to 2006's *Silent Hill*, in that it clearly understands and honours the source material on a visual and atmospheric level. Where it might fail game fans though, is with its curious changes to the story that, at times, can seem wholly unnecessary. The argument usually arises that video games and films are inherently different mediums and so the experience needs to be tweaked and streamlined, but with *Max Payne* already being such a cinematic game at heart, it seems a shame to not have adapted some of the game's more recognisable moments directly.

Max Payne (Mark Wahlberg) and Mona Sax (Mila Kunis) – © 20th Century Fox

A Valkyrie hallucination claiming a victim – © 20th Century Fox

Still, director John Moore knows what he is doing visually, as the movie sticks to its grey, snowy colour palette for the majority of scenes, drawing viewers further into the underbelly of society and, simultaneously, Max's fragile psyche.

Max Payne opened at number one at the box office and was a huge success, but it wasn't received well by critics.

WATCH IT FOR

The striking visuals and the intriguing duo of Mark Wahlberg and Mila Kunis.

SEQUEL?

While it was a huge monetary success and the video game spawned two sequels, no follow-up movie was developed.

Street Fighter:
The Legend of Chun-Li

RELEASE DATE
27 February 2009

DIRECTOR
Andrzej Bartkowiak

STARRING
Kristin Kreuk, Chris Klein, Neal McDonough

TAGLINE
"Some Fight for Power. Some Fight for Us"

Capcom's *Street Fighter* series had already seen a campy, big budget adaptation in 1994, but for this 2009 reimagining of the series the producers decided to focus on fan-favourite hero Chun-Li, as well as bringing a less comical approach to the material. Andrzej Barkowiak, who previously directed the 2005 adaptation of *Doom*, as well as martial arts hits *Romeo Must Die* and *Cradle 2 the Grave*, took the helm for this movie. Kristin Kreuk (*Smallville*) was cast in the lead role of Chun-Li and Neal McDonough (*Ravenous, Sonic the Hedgehog*) took the role of the villainous Bison.

Chun-Li is an aspiring pianist whose world is turned upside down when she is just a little girl. Having a close bond with her father, the businessman Huang Xiang (Edmund Chen), she spent some of her youth under his tutelage, learning the intricacies of the martial art, wushu. When her home is invaded by Bison and his thugs, Xiang is abducted, and Chun-Li and her mother are devastated. While she goes on to fulfil her wish of playing the piano, there is the nagging hint of uncertainty in her life as regards the fate of her father.

Bison's Shadaloo organization tightens its grip on the world, and the brutal leader eliminates both those who work for him and those who oppose him with reckless abandon. Following a mysterious message, Chun-Li heads to Bangkok, where she is mentored by the wise Gen (Robin Shou in his third role in a fighting game adaptation, having played Liu Kang in both *Mortal Kombat* movies and one of the goons who attacks Tina in *DOA: Dead or Alive*). Gen reveals his knowledge of

Left: Chun-Li in *Street Fighter IV* – © Capcom

Below: Chun-Li (Kristin Kreuk) in a predicament – © 20th Century Fox

both Shadaloo and the possible whereabouts of Chun-Li's father, leading her on a quest for answers and, more importantly, vengeance.

This adaptation of *Street Fighter* couldn't be further removed from the tone and spirit of the 1994 movie. For example, its story focuses on only a few characters from the video game series, namely the main hero and villain, the minions Balrog (the late Michael Clarke Duncan) and Vega (Black Eyed Peas

Bison (Neal McDonough) – © 20th Century Fox

member Taboo), and the Interpol agent Charlie Nash (Chris Klein) who tracks but eventually helps Chun-Li on her mission. The character of Charlie is known to be a friend of Guile's in the video game series, and in fact made an appearance in the 1994 movie, where he was brainwashed and transformed into the feral, green fighter, Blanka.

Despite the muted tone of the movie compared to the antics of the Van Damme flick, there is one comedic element that stands out, for perhaps the wrong reasons. Neal McDonough puts on an unconvincing accent as Bison is inexplicably given an Irish background. To be clear, McDonough himself does come from an Irish family, but it's obvious from the role he plays that the accent is not second nature to him. It's more *Darby O'Gill and the Little People* than anything you're likely to hear from a threatening and influential crime lord, and it's hard to deny how distracting it is when watching the movie.

> "When people are hungry, there's nothing they won't do."
>
> – Bison (Neal McDonough)

Kristin Kreuk actually makes for a likeable Chun-Li, so it's a shame that movie doesn't do her justice in many ways. Bartkowiak does a decent job as regards directing the fight choreography, but when the movie leaves so much to be desired in most of its other facets, the martial arts do little to get the blood pumping. While not completely abandoning some of the fantastical moves from the games, this film is definitely more concerned with being a martial arts movie played straight, rather than a cartoonish good time.

Street Fighter: The Legend of Chun-Li underperformed at the box office and was negatively received by critics.

WATCH IT FOR

The always brilliant Robin Shou as the iconic game character Gen, some decent choreography and to shake your head in disbelief at Neal McDonough's accent.

SEQUEL?

Unsurprisingly, no sequel ever came about for this ill-fated adaptation. The miniseries *Street Fighter: Assassin's Fist* would be the next time Street Fighter was brought into live action, and it was a hit with fans and critics.

Professor Layton and the Eternal Diva

RELEASE DATE
19 December 2009

DIRECTOR
Masakazu Hashimoto

STARRING THE VOICES OF
Christopher Robin Miller, Maria Darling, Emma Tate

TAGLINE
"Solve the Puzzle"

© Toho

With the runaway success of the Nintendo DS throughout the 2000s, it was nearly impossible to not have heard of the Professor Layton series. Following Layton and his young apprentice Luke, the adventure games tasked players with solving hundreds of puzzles, meticulously crafted to stump gamers around the world. These included maths problems, memory games and clever wordplay-based, 'whodunnit' style propositions. The series was one of the best-selling franchises on the DS, where it saw three installments, with another three prequels following on the Nintendo 3DS. The latest console release in the series was *Layton's Mystery Journey: Katrielle and the Millionaires' Conspiracy* (3DS, Mobile, Nintendo Switch), which starred the Professor's daughter instead.

It might not seem like the easiest type of game to bring to cinema given the nature of its gameplay, but the stellar animation found in the games lends itself effortlessly to the story on screen. When Luke and the professor are invited

Professor Layton and the Curious Village – © Level-5

by one of Layton's old students to watch an opera performance, they soon get more than they bargained for. They, along with a group of others who were attending, get drawn into a game that tests their wits and powers of deduction, with the winner being promised the gift of eternal life. Luckily for those attending, Professor Layton is ahead of the curve and a puzzle-solving mastermind, teaching his apprentice to consider all angles in the process. What seems like a bizarre competition slowly turns into a family matter with a powerful link to an ancient civilization.

Professor Layton and the Eternal Diva does as much as it possibly can to retain the atmosphere and humour of the game series. In lieu of letting viewers have direct control over the mysteries presented on screen, the film drip feeds the audience with hints, essentially allowing fans to make their own deductions along with the characters in the movie. Short of stopping the movie flat and speaking directly to the audience, like *Dora the Explorer*, it really is the best way of bringing Layton's brand of head-scratching puzzles to film.

The animation is crisp and beautiful, and the sweeping orchestral score is suitably epic. It also brings back some themes from the games, and players will be all too familiar with the highly-hummable accordion tunes from *Professor Layton and the Curious Village*. The voice acting is excellent too, with the actors playing Luke and Layton bringing an authenticity to the movie by reprising their roles.

"If the door to Ambrosia will not open by this music, I will tear it down!!"
– Jean Descole (Jonathan Keeble)

Luke (Maria Darling) and Professor Layton (Christopher Robin Miller) – © Toho

Melina (Emma Tate) – © Toho

There are some genuine twists to be found as the narrative thunders on, and some of the revelations Layton and others discover can be really satisfying to attempt to crack, as a viewer. There's a heartfelt, and oftentimes tragic story weaving through the movie, but Layton's understanding of humanity makes him a fantastic anchor. The movie also contains some visually amazing virtual sets, from the opera house to the woods on a mysterious island, and the climax takes place by the sea for an incredible battle of wits that really shows the quality of the animation on offer.

It's hard to deny the charm of Professor Layton's first film outing and it should be priority viewing for anyone with a love for the charming world of puzzle solving.

Professor Layton and the Eternal Diva was released to positive reviews and box office success.

WATCH IT FOR

A story full of genuine emotion, clever brain teasers, wonderful animation and a catchy soundtrack.

SEQUEL?

No film sequel has manifested yet, but the Layton franchise has continued on screen with the anime series *Layton Mystery Detective Agency*, which lasted for fifty episodes from 2018–2019.

The Best of the Rest – 2000s

The *Pokémon* film series continued throughout the decade, along with a number of other animated works based on successful gaming franchises. *Sin: The Movie*, based on the first-person shooter franchise, was released in 2000, loosely adapting the game. An animated prequel to the mech-shooter *Zone of the Enders*, entitled *Zone of the Enders: 2167 Idolo* was released in 2001, to a warm critical reception.

From the mid-2000s onwards, a number of massive gaming franchises made their way to the small screen. The *Metal Gear Solid* and *Metal Gear Solid 2 Digital Novels* were released, bringing the motion comics to home video. The *Street Fighter Alpha* series saw an anime movie adaptation with *Street Fighter Alpha: Generations,* which saw a western release as part of the bonus features on the DVD of *Street Fighter: The Legend of Chun-Li.*

A live-action film based on the popular *Yakuza* series was released in 2007, and followed a similar premise to the original game in the series, with robberies and brutal fights in Kamurocho, a fictitious Tokyo district. It was titled *Yakuza: Like a Dragon* (not to be confused with the 2020 video game of the same name).

In 2007, the massively popular *The King of Kong: A Fistful of Quarters* documentary movie was released. It followed the endearing story of a back-and-forth battle between two men, Steve Wiebe and Billy Mitchell, as both fought to regain and retain their high scores on the original 1981 *Donkey Kong* arcade game. Similarly, *Chasing Ghosts: Beyond the Arcade* was released in 2007 and chronicled the impact of the golden age of arcade video games.

A live-action film of the popular Japanese hack-and-slash series *OneChanbara* was released in 2008, and followed the premise of the games, with scantily-clad cowgirl Aya facing hordes of zombies and demons.

Two animated movies based on the sci-fi survival-horror series *Dead Space* were released in 2008 and 2011. They were *Dead Space: Downfall* and *Dead Space: Aftermath,* and both dealt with the terrifying Necromorphs attempting to murder the crews of various spaceships and stations.

In 2009, renowned English satirist Charlie Brooker, known for his sci-fi drama anthology series *Black Mirror,* released a video game themed show called *Gameswipe*. It was similar in structure to his TV review series *Screenwipe* and his news review series *Newswipe,* and was a satirical and informative one-off special showing the workings of the video game industry, as well as its follies. It also showcased several popular games and consoles, all with Brooker's trademark, deadpan humour.

The King of Fighters

RELEASE DATE
7 September 2010

DIRECTOR
Gordon Chan

STARRING
Sean Faris,
Maggie Q,
Ray Park

© Arclight Films

Along with Capcom's *Street Fighter* series, Japanese developer SNK carved out their own legion of one-on-one fighting fans with its *King of Fighters* series. Now standing at fifteen main entries, the series brought team battles to the fighting game scene, allowing players to choose three characters with which to achieve victory. Hoping to win the tournament and coveted title of the King of Fighters, trained warriors such as Kyo, Terry and Iori fight in intense battles with a massive roster of playable fighters; and the otherworldly Rugal, an ominous and over-powered, callous human who usually serves as a final boss and who has surely led to masses of controllers being chucked across living rooms in frustration.

Like *Street Fighter: The Legend of Chun-Li*, the film adaptation of *The King of Fighters* tries to mesh some of the otherworldly nature of the games with a modern-day sensibility, while downplaying the colourful nature of the video games. The characters are invited to an inter-dimensional battle through the use of Bluetooth headsets, where the malicious Rugal (Ray Park – *Star Wars Episode I: The Phantom Menace, X-Men*) attempts to defeat them. Franchise staples Mai (Maggie Q – *Divergent* series, *Designated Survivor, Live Free or Die Hard*), her boyfriend Iori (Will Yun Lee – *Witchblade, Die Another Day, Elektra*) and series hero Kyo Kusanagi (Sean Faris – *Pearl Harbor, Pretty Little Liars*) must work together, along with agent Terry Bogard, in order to solve Rugal's puzzling plan and defeat him.

Kyo has a lineage as yet unknown to him, and Mai helps him to figure out where his destiny lies in relation to the burden of his family heritage. Terry questions nearly every move the group make, preferring to take the logical route over a belief in magic powers and alternate dimensions. It isn't long before he's whisked into the fray however, and the group band together to use their strengths in an attempt to defeat the evil demon-like human.

The King of Fighters is only for absolute die-hards of the series, and even then, it's a massive toss up as to whether they'll enjoy it or not. Like the 2009 *Street Fighter* movie or 2008's *Far Cry*, the movie could have played out more or less the same without the *King of Fighters* branding or

The King of Fighters '96 – © SNK

**Kyo Kusanagi (Sean Faris) –
© Arclight Films**

Mai (Maggie Q) – © Arclight Films

characters. At some point in the development of these movies the question was surely asked if there was anything other than brand recognition behind the inclusion of the titles or characters.

Given Ray Park's athletic skill there is definitely *some* enjoyment to be gained from the fight scenes, but overall, the movie feels disconnected from its source and seems content to plod along with questionable dialogue and multiple changes in pace to allow for exposition.

It's not surprising that the movie passed most gamers by without them even being aware of its existence. But, like some of Uwe Boll's work, it's bound to have late-night watchers who view it as background noise or want to enjoy it ironically.

The King of Fighters was panned and failed at the box office.

WATCH IT FOR

Ray Park's choreography and Terry Bogard's (David Leitch) sarcastic one-liners.

SEQUEL?

Unsurprisingly, no sequel was made for this arcade adaptation.

Tekken

RELEASE DATE
20 March 2010

DIRECTOR
Dwight H. Little

STARRING
Jon Foo, Kelly Overton, Cary-Hiroyuki Tagawa

TAGLINE
"Survival is No Game"

Oᵉ ne of the prominent 3D fighting games of the '90s, alongside others such as *Virtua Fighter* and *Battle Arena Toshinden*, Namco's *Tekken* made its impact in arcades as well as at home, on Sony's PlayStation console. Players could choose from traditional martial artists such as Jin, Xiaoyu and Lee as well as more fantastical characters like the sword-wielding ninjitsu expert Yoshimitsu, the robotic fighter Jack and the huge grizzly bear, Kuma. With the series at seven main installments as of 2021, it has been a huge success for Namco, with its innovative character design and satisfying grapple move mechanics.

A film adaptation arrived in 2010, under the direction of Dwight H. Little. For this movie iteration, Jin Kazama, a prominent character in the ongoing storyline of the games, takes the lead, living in the slums outside Tekken city and taking on illegal shipment jobs for those in need of money and food. When the Jackhammers, an elite guard used to protect the wealthy, break into his home and kill his mother, Jin vows for revenge. When he finds out about the King of Iron Fist tournament, he sees it as a way to get closer to Heihachi Mishima (Cary-Hiroyuki Tagawa in his second villainous role in a fighting franchise adaptation, after playing the evil sorcerer Shang Tsung in 1995's *Mortal Kombat*), the leader of a massive corporation and owner of the Jackhammers.

Once he gains entry to the tournament, Jin must climb his way through the rounds, facing skilled fighters and contending with the ever-watchful eyes of Heihachi's son, Kazuya. All is not as it seems as the tournament rages on, and as it reaches its conclusion, the stakes turn deadly.

Tekken takes a lot of liberties with the series it's based on. While many fan favourites are present, albeit altered from their gaming counterparts, there are a number of bizarre decisions story-wise that seem wholly unnecessary. Still, being a video game adaptation this should hardly be surprising, as *Super Mario Bros.* set the bar high (low??) as regards how you can interpret a gaming franchise on screen. The fights are varied throughout the movie, whether it's the smooth capoeira of Eddy Gordo or the deadly sword play of the always intriguing Yoshimitsu.

> "I am Mishima Heihachi. I am Tekken. You will fail."
> – Heihachi Mishima (Cary-Hiroyuki Tagawa)

Tekken 2 – © Namco

Left: Jin Kazama (Jon Foo) – © Anchor Bay Entertainment

Below: Some combatants in the King of Iron Fist Tournament – © Anchor Bay Entertainment

While most of the battles take place on a singular stage in the tournament arena, the filmmakers decided to bring the stage select option onto film, and the battleground can be altered to mimic a number of different locations. It's an odd but brave choice that stops the movie from becoming yet another globe-trotting action flick.

Tekken is far from the worst video game movie, but again it feels as though the names and brand have been tacked on to what could have been its own martial arts action movie. Die-hard fans might get a kick out of the myriad of characters on show, particularly Eddy, Christie and Yoshimitsu (newer additions to the gaming series, such as Raven and Dragunov also appear, faithfully recreated) but the movie lacks the proper punch needed to make this a definitive adaptation of *Tekken*.

Tekken wasn't received well critically and lacked success at the box office.

WATCH IT FOR

Some faithful character recreations, a few entertaining fights and Cary-Hiroyuki Tagawa as Heihachi Mishima.

SEQUEL?

A prequel, entitled *Tekken 2: Kazuya's Revenge* was released in 2014, with Wych Kaos taking on directing duties. Cary-Hiroyuki Tagawa returned as Heihachi and Gary Daniels returned as the half-cyborg combatant, Bryan Fury. Like its predecessor, it was not well received.

Prince of Persia: The Sands of Time

RELEASE DATE
28 May 2010

DIRECTOR
Mike Newell

STARRING
Jake Gyllenhaal,
Gemma Arterton,
Ben Kingsley

TAGLINE
"Defy the Future"

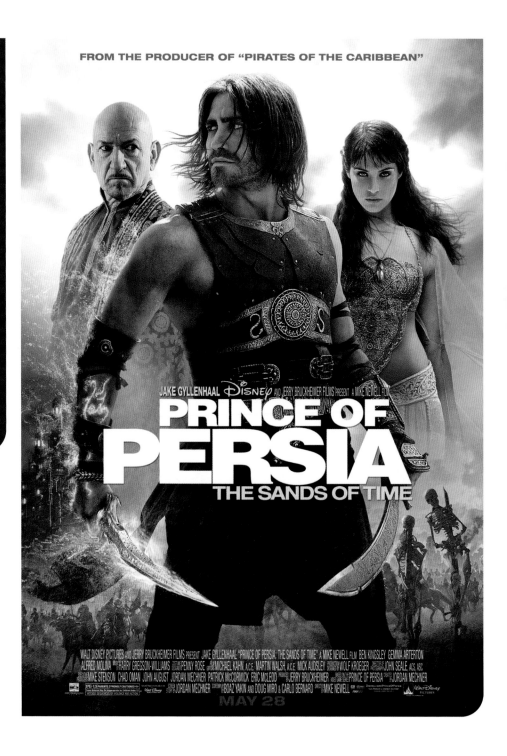

PRINCE OF PERSIA: THE SANDS OF TIME

Following the massive success of the original *Pirates of the Caribbean* trilogy, producer Jerry Bruckheimer sought to recreate the adventurous nature of those films with an adaptation of the 2003 video game *Prince of Persia: The Sands of Time* (PS2, Xbox, GameCube). This game was actually the fourth in the series, and a reimagining of the franchise. It saw an unnamed prince gain control of the Dagger of Time, which contained mystical sands that could reverse time and alter the fate of those who wielded it. He tries to use this power to stop an evil Vizier from ruling the kingdom.

The game featured engaging combat, a well-written and well-acted story and athletic parkour-style traversal. A huge hit for the PlayStation 2, Xbox and GameCube, it re-established *Prince of Persia* as a pioneer in the action-adventure genre. Two successful sequels followed, along with another installment that took place in the middle of the trilogy (*Prince of Persia: The Forgotten Sands*).

The film was released in 2010 and was directed by Mike Newell, known for directing *Harry Potter and the Goblet of Fire*, the fourth entry in the blockbuster *Wizarding World* franchise. He's once again able to use that sense of scale here, as *Prince of Persia* is a pure cinematic blockbuster. Following the adventures of the titular hero, named Dastan for this adaptation, it took a few liberties with the story of the game, but nevertheless keeps its spirit intact.

Prince of Persia: The Sands of Time – © Ubisoft

Prince Nizam (Ben Kingsley), Dastan (Jake Gyllenhaal) and Prince Tus (Richard Coyle) – © Walt Disney Pictures

Dastan, a homeless urchin who is adopted by the king, takes part in a siege of the city of Alamut. The prince and the Persian army are attempting to stop the forging of weapons for opposing forces, but instead Dastan procures a dagger from one of the guards. After he is framed for murder, Dastan flees the city with the Princess of Alamut, Tamina (Gemma Arterton – *St Trinian's, Hansel & Gretel: Witch Hunters, Clash of the Titans*). While on the run, Dastan discovers the nature of the dagger and its time-travelling abilities. When Dastan and Tamina uncover a plot by Prince Nizam (Ben Kingsley – *Gandhi, BloodRayne*), they set out to stop him from carrying out his grave plans.

"All the pain in the world will not help you find something that does not exist."
– Princess Tamina (Gemma Arterton)

The Sands of Time is a low-commitment, fast-paced adventure film. With its intriguing premise and gorgeous setting, its production value alone sets it in the higher echelons of video game adaptations. Featuring a story that was developed by the creator of the game franchise, Jordan Mechner, and genuine chemistry between Jake Gyllenhaal and Gemma Arterton, the movie should please fans of the 2003 video game and casual viewers alike.

The flirty, sarcastic exchanges between the Dastan and Princess Tamina evoke the game directly, and the brilliantly choreographed parkour and fight scenes are faithful to the rebooted trilogy on which the film is based. The time-travel plot device is mostly put to good use, and these sequences are satisfying to watch, with dreamy special effects as the fabric of time is torn asunder.

Prince Dastan (Jake Gyllenhaal) and Princess Tamina (Gemma Arterton) – © Walt Disney Studios

There is a healthy amount of humour to the proceedings, in particular when Sheik Amar (Alfred Molina – *Raiders of the Lost Ark, Spider-Man 2*) makes his appearance. He attempts to keep the princess and Dastan imprisoned and claim the reward for their capture. Their escape, involving a high-stakes ostrich racecourse, is one of the more ludicrous scenes in the movie, but it provides a jolt of comic relief amongst the epic battles and time-bending shenanigans.

Prince of Persia: The Sands of Time got mixed reviews from critics, but at the time of its release it became the highest-grossing movie based on a video game.

WATCH IT FOR

The authentic story developed by the game's creator, the innovative time-reversal plot device and the combination of visually arresting cinematography and choreography.

SEQUEL?

Despite the box office draw and the potential for the prince's adventures given the wealth of game content to draw from, no sequel materialised.

Resident Evil: Afterlife

RELEASE DATE
10 September 2010

DIRECTOR
Paul W.S. Anderson

STARRING
Milla Jovovich,
Ali Larter,
Wentworth Miller

TAGLINE
"Experience A
New Dimension
of Evil"

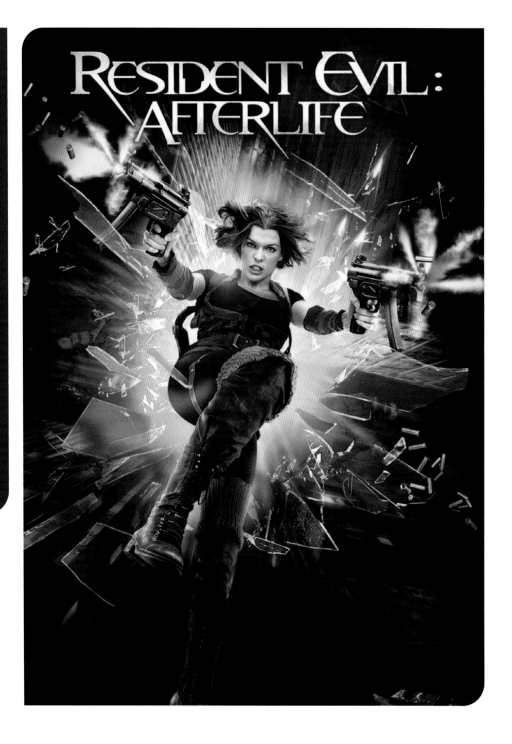

Paul W.S. Anderson returned to the blockbuster franchise in a directorial role for the first time since the 2002 original with *Resident Evil: Afterlife*.

Four years after the outbreak of the T-virus, ex-Umbrella employee Alice is still crossing the globe on her seemingly never-ending mission to stop the evil corporation's plans once and for all. Having gained more understanding of the powers within her, she aids survivors on their journey to a supposed safe haven called Arcadia.

Of course, the pilgrimage could never be that simple, and the group come across the usual mutations as well as a whole host of new, deadly creatures. The mutated Cerberus dogs with heads quite literally full of teeth are a force to be reckoned with, as is the abomination known as the Executioner, as seen in the video game *Resident Evil 5*.

Other elements from *Resident Evil 5* are adapted in this installment too, such as unnerving 'Las Plagas' type of enemies from the game series, whose mouths split apart to reveal tendrils with rows of razor-sharp teeth. Likewise, the ruby scarabs that can control the host they're attached to make an appearance.

Franchise veteran Claire Redfield returns, with Ali Larter reprising her role from *Extinction*. This time she is joined by one of the heroes of the original game; her brother

Right: **The Executioner from *Resident Evil 5* – © Capcom**

Below: **Alice (Milla Jovovich) – © Sony Pictures Releasing**

Claire (Ali Larter) and Chris
Redfield (Wentworth Miller) –
© Sony Pictures Releasing

Chris (Wentworth Miller – *Prison Break, Legends of Tomorrow*). Miller is stoic and sarcastic as Chris, but an effective force to be reckoned with when it comes to dealing with the infected. The group initially don't trust him, having incarcerated him, but he has more than enough opportunities throughout the movie to prove himself.

Milla Jovovich and her character, Alice, seem to only grow with confidence with each sequel in the series. Alice's arc is one filled with doubt and often, hopelessness. Yet just as often she shows a serenity and control over her mind, the situation and her powers. The movie is jam-packed with action, from Alice's hand-to-hand precision to Claire and Chris' adept use of firearms. It doesn't skimp on the slow-mo either, gleefully revelling in the special effects and most probably looking for ways to use the 3D effect that was seeing a resurgence around the time of the film's release.

> "I'm what you used to be, only better."
> – Albert Wesker (Shawn Roberts)

With another healthy mix of gory action and slow, atmospheric moments, Anderson honours certain elements of the game series while continuing to carve his own path for the blockbuster franchise.

Resident Evil: Afterlife wasn't well received by critics, but like the previous movies in the series, it was a massive box office success.

WATCH IT FOR

The stylish opening credits scene, the best soundtrack in the series so far, composed by duo Tomandandy, and the numerous elements of the game that are incorporated into the narrative.

SEQUEL?

Yes, Anderson and Jovovich returned for another sequel in 2012, *Resident Evil: Retribution*.

Resident Evil: Retribution

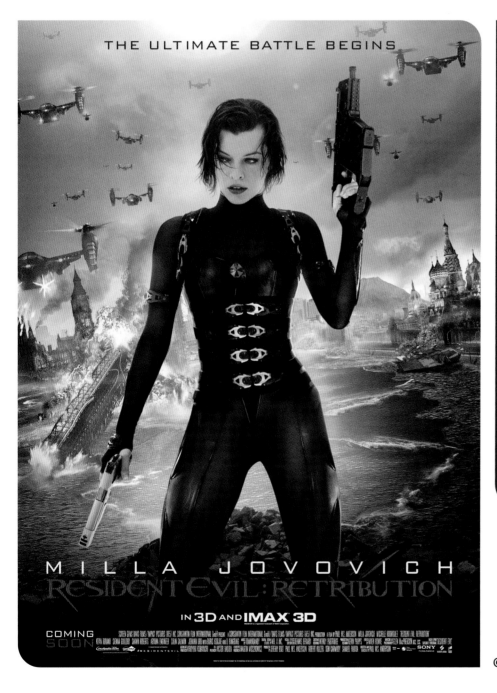

© Sony Pictures Releasing

RELEASE DATE
14 September 2012

DIRECTOR
Paul W.S. Anderson

STARRING
Milla Jovovich, Michelle Rodriguez, Sienna Guillory

TAGLINE
"The Ultimate Battle Begins"

Ten years after the release of the original movie, Paul Anderson wrote and directed the fifth film in the action-horror series. It's by far the most 'out there' entry, and that's saying something when your franchise consists of six films following dozens of different kinds of mutated beasts destroying mankind as we know it.

Milla Jovovich returns as Alice, the formidable thorn in the side of the Umbrella Corporation, in particular their calculating leader, Albert Wesker. Picking up where *Afterlife* left off, Alice finds herself held captive by Umbrella, where she is subjected to a bizarre series of situations that see her confront the ghosts of her past, quite literally in some cases. The film is to be commended for mixing up the formula at least a little bit, throwing quite a few curve balls that are sure to keep the audience questioning the realities they're seeing play out on screen. In this way, the movie acts like a sort of 'greatest hits' of the series thus far and, arguably, ends up being the movie that seems most comparable to a video game.

Adding to the growing roster of famous faces seen in each movie so far, Anderson brings one of the most recognisable heroes from the game series, Leon S. Kennedy, into the fold. Not content with just that, *Retribution* goes heavy on the fan service by adding the devious Ada Wong and the loveable Barry Burton to the group of saviours trying to take down Wesker's tyrannical operation.

Sienna Guillory makes her return to the series for the first time since 2004's *Apocalypse* (save for a mid-credits cameo in *Afterlife*), but she is not as Alice remembers her. The inclusion of multiple characters from previous entries surprisingly touches on some heavy nostalgic vibes, particularly if you had been following this series since its inception in 2002.

Following these well-known characters through ludicrous set pieces makes the movie's hour and a half run time fly by, and fans of the previous movies should have their action appetite truly whet by this installment. Anderson really throws everything at this adaptation, with a plethora of creatures, returning characters and weapons assaulting the senses with little room for a breath. As well as the usual slow-mo shootouts, the hand-to-hand and

Jill Valentine in *Resident Evil 5* – © Capcom

Jill Valentine (Sienna Guillory) – © Sony Pictures Releasing

Leon S. Kennedy (Johann Urb) and Ada Wong (Li Bingbing) – © Sony Pictures Releasing

weapon combat has been upped heavily, ensuring there are plenty of ferocious fights, particularly at the climax, which is an all-out brawl.

> "What is this? What have you done to me?"
>
> – Alice (Milla Jovovich)

The film, of course, sets up another movie, as the journey of Alice has not quite reached its conclusion.

There were some good reviews for *Resident Evil: Retribution*, praising its action scenes and its similarities to a video game in general. It was a huge success at the box office.

WATCH IT FOR

Series icons Leon, Barry and Ada play large roles in the movie, and it's nice to see more ties to the games. The fight choreography is tight and exciting, and seeing returning characters from the previous movies helps set up the next, and last, *Resident Evil* movie.

SEQUEL?

Yes, Paul Anderson and his wife Milla Jovovich returned in 2017 for *Resident Evil: The Final Chapter*, the swansong for the series that had been tearing up the box office for 15 years. It would see the end of Alice's journey, and wrap up the story of Umbrella and their brutal and apocalyptic T-virus.

Silent Hill: Revelation (3D)

RELEASE DATE
26 October 2012

DIRECTOR
Michael J. Bassett

STARRING
Adelaide Clemens, Kit Harington, Carrie-Anne Moss

TAGLINE
"This Halloween, Prepare for a 3D Ride Through Hell"

SILENT HILL: REVELATION (3D)

Six years after Rose Da Silva's journey through hell, the psychological horror franchise returned to the big screen for *Silent Hill: Revelation*. With a heavily 3D-focused marketing campaign, it sought to visually dazzle with more of the disturbing creature design and striking imagery of the first movie.

The film mainly adapts the video game *Silent Hill 3* (2003 – PS2, PC and PS3/Xbox 360 as part of *Silent Hill HD Collection* in 2012), featuring a now-adult Sharon Da Silva, living her life under her new identity, Heather Mason. Her father, Christopher (Sean Bean), now goes by Harry, and the two have tried to move on with their lives after the harrowing events of the original film. It isn't long however, before Heather is drawn to the town to confront her own dark past.

Joining her is Vincent (Kit Harrington – *Game of Thrones, Pompeii, Spooks: The Greater Good*), a man with a tie to the Order that dwell in the town and have their own insidious practices at play. Christopher/Harry is this time drawn into the fray, and is finally shown the true horrors of *Silent Hill* as he witnesses the disturbing Otherworld, a hellscape of twisted metal, deadly creatures and psychological torment.

Silent Hill: Revelation is shorter and more streamlined than the exposition-heavy original. Akira Yamaoka's atmospheric soundtrack (lifted from the video games) once again serves to punctuate the horror, and Michael J. Bassett shows a deft hand at pacing as the film zips through set piece after set piece. It's definitely more style over substance this time around for *Silent Hill*, but fans of disturbing creatures like the faceless nurses, the legendary Pyramid

Silent Hill 3 – © **Konami**

Vincent (Kit Harington) and Heather (Adelaide Clemens) – © Open Road Films

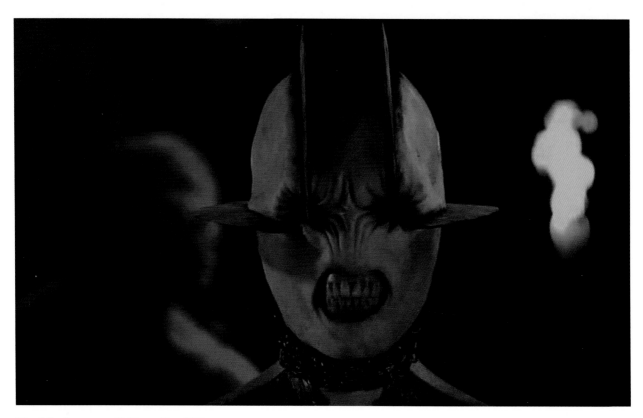

The Missionary – © Open Road Films

Head and a bizarre beast composed entirely of pieces of mannequin dolls should feel right at home in what essentially equates to a haunted house attraction come to life.

With a climax set in a twisted amusement park, *Silent Hill: Revelation* tries its best to adapt the more memorable sets and moments from *Silent Hill 3*. If you enjoyed the first movie it's hard to imagine that you wouldn't get something from this sequel, but in many ways it's a different beast, mostly in terms of the depth of its story and characters.

If you're content to join a horror rollercoaster with little let up, it will probably be up your alley. *Silent Hill: Revelation* was a moderate box office success but didn't fare well with critics who lamented how one-dimensional it was, which is ironic given its otherworldly premise.

"Go to hell!"

– Heather Mason (Adelaide Clemens)

"Can't you see? We're already here..."

– Alessa Gillespie

WATCH IT FOR

As always, Akira Yamaoka's score, but also for authentic creature design that honours the games as well as a cameo from *Silent Hill: Origins* (2007 – PSP, PS2) protagonist, Travis Grady.

SEQUEL?

No sequel has yet materialised, but the director of the original move, Christophe Gans, recently casually revealed he was beginning work on a new *Silent Hill* movie.

Need for Speed

RELEASE DATE
14 March 2014

DIRECTOR
Scott Waugh

STARRING
Aaron Paul,
Dominic Cooper,
Michael Keaton

© Walt Disney Studios

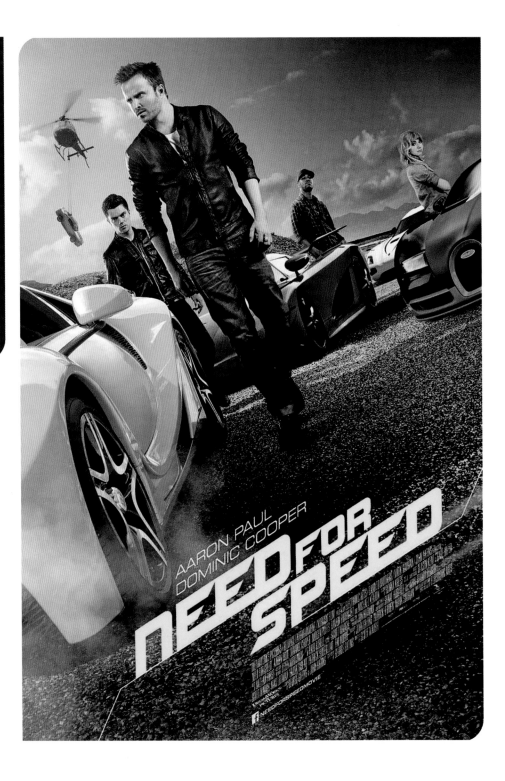

The *Need for Speed* franchise has been providing players with high-octane thrills for over 25 years. The initial title, *The Need for Speed*, was praised for its realism and thrilling pace. The franchise has evolved over the decades, mainly focusing on street racing and evading the pursuit of law enforcement through breakneck chases, but it has also expanded to include simulations, like the *Shift* sub-series of games.

Like *Ridge Racer, Gran Turismo* and the *Burnout* series, *Need for Speed* has been massively successful, selling hundreds of millions of copies across a plethora of gaming platforms. Given the box office draw of franchises like the *Fast & Furious* series, it made sense for *Need for Speed* to come to the silver screen in some form. In 2014, Scott Waugh took the wheel and directed an adaptation which saw Aaron Paul (*Breaking Bad, BoJack Horseman, Exodus: Gods and Kings*) play the lead role of mechanic Tobey Marshall.

Tobey and his friends make their living repairing cars, but by night they participate in illegal street races to try and bring in some much-needed extra cash. When Tobey's rival, Dino Brewster (Dominic Cooper – *Preacher, Warcraft*), gives the crew a fix-up job that could see them bring in big bucks, Tobey reluctantly agrees. Things don't exactly go to plan however, and a seemingly harmless attempt to squeeze a little more cash out of the opportunity leads to a series of tragic events. Tobey then sets out on a journey for redemption, which throws him and his crew into all manner of thrilling, country-spanning car chases. He shares parts of his journey with Julia (Imogen Poots – *28 Weeks Later, The Look of Love, Fright Night*), who is made to accompany Tobey as he drives an expensive Mustang to enter a high-stakes underground race called De Leon. The race is run by Monarch (Michael Keaton – *Batman, Beetlejuice, Birdman, Multiplicity*), a farm-dwelling man who is initially suspicious of Tobey's notoriety.

On paper, this movie does all it should need to do to satisfy fans of chase movies. Waugh directs the action well, and Aaron Paul is a really likeable protagonist. But the disconnect between player and viewer means that this could really be any car chase film, and it's fairly

Need for Speed: Hot Pursuit – © **Electronic Arts**

Julia (Imogen Poots) and Tobey (Aaron Paul) – © Walt Disney Studios

© Walt Disney Studios

obvious that the title will be the main draw for audiences. A popcorn movie through and through, those expecting anything more will be sorely disappointed. It's got heart, it's got speed and it's got a decent collection of likeable, if clichéd characters. At the very least it might have viewers itching to get behind the wheel (or controller) themselves.

> "We'll settle this behind the wheel."
> – Tobey Marshall (Aaron Paul)

Need for Speed was a big success at the box office, but it didn't fare well with critics.

WATCH IT FOR

Aaron Paul and Dominic Cooper's rivalry, the cars and some genuinely great car chase scenes.

SEQUEL?

A sequel has been spoken about and appears to be planned, but there has been no further news regarding it to date.

Hitman: Agent 47

RELEASE DATE
21 August 2015

DIRECTOR
Aleksander Bach

STARRING
Rupert Friend,
Hannah Ware,
Zachary Quinto

TAGLINE
"Your Number is
Up"

Agent 47 made his return to cinema in 2015, with a reboot entitled *Hitman: Agent 47*, that saw British actor Rupert Friend (*Homeland, The Boy in the Striped Pyjamas, The French Dispatch*) take on the role of the mysterious and deadly assassin. German director Aleksander Bach took the helm this time around, in a movie that has a more streamlined and less convoluted approach than the 2007 film. There is more of a focus on action in this adaptation, and Agent 47 is played with a straight and robotic poise by Friend, tapping into the hitman's dutiful, unfeeling nature.

Hannah Ware (*Boss, Betrayal, Oldboy*) co-stars as Katia van Dees, a character with arguably more importance to the plot than the hitman himself. She is searching for her father, who has ties to the Agent program that created 47, and after a few initial near-fatal encounters, the two work together to evade a number of dangers, including the relentless pursuit of John Smith (Zachary Quinto – *Heroes, Star Trek*), a super-powered member of Syndicate, a group who are trying to stop Agent 47. Katia and 47 unearth the whereabouts of her father, leading to a cacophony of bullets and fist-fights.

"Do you know what makes you weak? You wanting to prove that you are better than me."

– Agent 47 (Rupert Friend)

"Ok, untie me."

– Katia (Hannah Ware)

"You're the same as me, so untie yourself."

– Agent 47

Hitman: Absolution – © IO Interactive

Agent 47 (Rupert Friend) and Katia (Hannah Ware) – © 20th Century Fox

Shaking up the tone was probably for the best for this series. That's not to say that the politically-charged original didn't work, but there is something satisfying about seeing this version of Agent 47 being unleashed, his nature remaining unfazed as he and Katia work their way through dozens of Syndicate henchmen in search of the truth. While the

Agent 47 (Rupert Friend) – © 20th Century Fox

fast-paced choreography might be at odds with the mostly slow and stealthy approach of the video games, there's no denying that some of the scenes here are spectacular action showcases.

The climax - which sees 47 and Katia infiltrate a Syndicate skyscraper - is fairly unrelenting and should give fans and casual viewers alike a few reasons to fist-pump the air with satisfaction. All in all, those in the need for a solid action movie should find some popcorn thrills in Agent 47's rebooted outing.

Hitman: Agent 47 was a modest box office success but didn't fare well with critics.

WATCH IT FOR

Rupert Friend's emotionless performance, and Hannah Ware's emotional one, some pulse-pounding action, and a scene in which Katia pilots a helicopter straight through the front of a building.

SEQUEL?

Given the critical response to the movie, it's unlikely that a sequel to this iteration will ever be made. Agent 47 is surely going to return to the screen in some form in the future, especially given the massive success of 2021's *Hitman III* (PS4, Xbox One, Nintendo Switch (Cloud), PC).

Ratchet & Clank

RELEASE DATE
29 April 2016

DIRECTOR
Kevin Munroe

STARRING THE VOICES OF
James Arnold Taylor, David Kaye, Sylvester Stallone

TAGLINE
"Kick Some Asteroid"

*R*atchet & Clank became household names throughout the 2000s, with a series of hit platforming games on Sony's PlayStation 2 and PlayStation 3 systems. Featuring a cat-like 'lombax' and his mechanical sidekick, the series was innovative for its use of novelty weaponry, and saw Ratchet wield a number of inspired and hilarious guns in order to defeat his enemies. These include, but are not limited to; the Ryno, the Quack-O-Ray, the Bouncer and the Seeker. Together with his friend and a robust arsenal, Ratchet took part in many adventures that involved precise platforming and original, gun-based combat. It was one of two Sony exclusive franchises that focused on sci-fi heavy aesthetics, storylines and weapons, the other being Naughty Dog's hugely successful *Jak & Daxter* series.

Following the eighth main entry, *Ratchet & Clank: Into the Nexus* (2013 – PS3), it was decided by development team Insomniac Games, that the series should be re-imagined for the next iteration. At this time, a feature-length, theatrical film was also green-lit. The 2016 game, simply titled *Ratchet & Clank*, was developed in conjunction with the movie of the same name. The animators and developers were in touch over story elements, visual designs and characters.

As such, the movie is as safe as you can expect. Following the mechanic Ratchet, who longs to join the Galactic Rangers who work to protect the galaxy from insidious forces, including the evil Chairman Drek, he soon finds that his idol, Captain Quark, is egotistical and denies Ratchet a chance to join based on his unsavoury past. Eventually, after teaming up with a robot named Clank, who, through an assembly line malfunction became good rather than evil,

Ratchet & Clank (PS4 - 2016) – © **Sony Computer Entertainment**

Clank (David Kaye) and Ratchet (James Arnold Taylor) – © Gramercy Pictures

Chairman Drek (Paul Giamatti) and Lieutenant Victor Von Ion (Sylvester Stallone) – © Gramercy Pictures

Ratchet stops a robot force from attacking civilians and destroying the city. Quark then has little choice but to let the lombax join the Rangers as their fifth member.

Ratchet & Clank knows what it wants to be. Part comedy, part science fiction adventure, the movie throws enough one-liners and slapstick at viewers to keep them modestly entertained for the sub-two hour run time. Some of the exposition-heavy scenes might bore really young viewers, but with Ratchet's heart, Clank's dry wit and Quark's ridiculous ego, it should manage a good few chuckles from the audience. The animation on show here is stellar, with vibrant worlds and characters, and hopefully, for fans of the game series, seeing the unlikely duo on screen will be worth the price of admission.

"Blaming yourself and taking responsibility are two very different things."

– Clank (David Kaye)

Ratchet & Clank was a box office disappointment and did not fare well critically.

WATCH IT FOR

The top-notch animation, great vocal performances and sci-fi aesthetic that's easy on the eyes.

SEQUEL?

No sequel has arrived yet for this feature, and given its performance, it seems unlikely it ever will. The game series thunders on, with the lombax and robot most recently teaming up for *Ratchet & Clank: Rift Apart* for the PlayStation 5 in 2021.

The Angry Birds Movie

RELEASE DATE
20 May 2016

DIRECTOR
Clay Kaytis &
Fergal Reilly

**STARRING THE
VOICES OF**
Jason Sudeikis,
Josh Gad, Danny
McBride

The rise of mobile apps and the ease of access to them opened up gaming to a whole new audience. Quick and addictive was the name of the game for many high-profile releases, with titles like the *Candy Crush* series and *Flappy Bird* becoming worldwide phenomenons through their low-commitment play sessions and simple to understand gameplay. At the height of the mobile revolution, came *Angry Birds*. This stylish and addictive game saw players catapulting a variety of birds, each with different strengths and styles, at structures housing the mischievous green piggies, who have stolen the birds' eggs.

The series was a massive success, reaching a mind-boggling four billion downloads as of 2020. With its addictive and more-ish gameplay, it didn't take long for the franchise to expand, bringing swathes of merchandise, crossover versions of the series including the *Star Wars* and *Transformers* franchises and, of course, a feature-length film. While their escapades had previously been chronicled in the series *Angry Birds Toons* (2013–2016), the colourful birds and their enemies had yet to make the leap to the big screen. Long-time animators and first-time directors Clay Kaytis and Fergal Reilly were chosen to direct an animated film of *Angry Birds*, and it features an all-star voice cast comprising some of modern comedy's most famous and versatile stars.

Jason Sudeikis voices Red, a short-tempered outcast who has consistently been on the outside compared to his feathered neighbours. At an anger management class, Red comes across Chuck (Josh Gad – *Frozen, Pixels, Beauty and the Beast*), a mindlessly optimistic yellow bird who desperately tries to be his friend, and Bomb (Danny McBride – *Pineapple Express, Eastbound & Down, Alien: Covenant*), a shy but loveable bird with a pre-disposition for exploding when under intense stress.

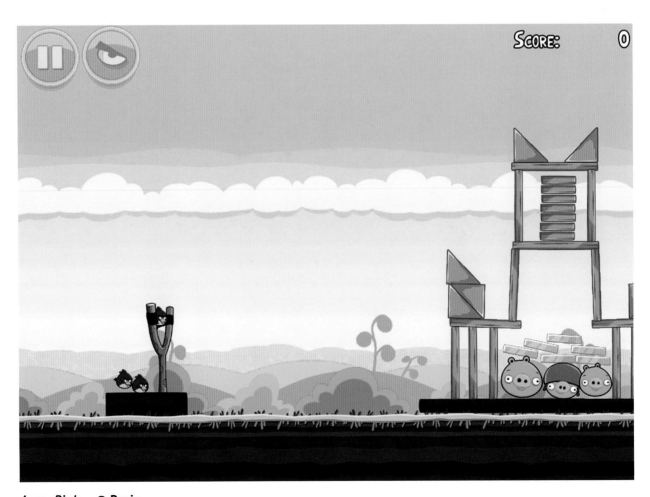

Angry Birds – © Rovio

Red (Jason Sudeikis) – © Sony Pictures Releasing

When a boat of green piggies led by a large pig called Leonard (Bill Hader – *Saturday Night Live, Trainwreck, It: Chapter Two*) docks on Bird Island, Red is dubious as to their motives, although they claim to have arrived in peace. Red's worries prove to be legitimate, and soon he, Chuck and Bomb must journey to find the Mighty Eagle (Peter Dinklage – *Game of Thrones*, *The Station Agent*, *X-Men: Days of Future Past*) who they believe can help them stop the bad piggies in their tracks.

"Hey, you know what? I used to believe in you. When I was a kid I believed nothing really bad could ever happen because you were here. And now I see the fate of the world hangs on idiots like me. And that, sir, is sort of terrifying."

– Red (Jason Sudeikis)

Leonard (Bill Hader) – © Sony Pictures Releasing

Being based on such a simple premise, the movie deserves kudos for both staying true to the birds' powers and nature and expanding the story with a diverse cast of genuinely likeable characters. The main trio of Sudeikis, Gad and McBride is a winner, and their back-and-forths are sure to have kids and adults laughing in equal measure. There are plenty of nods to the games, with the final act of the movie bringing the app's massive slingshots into the fold for a memorable climax.

While the movie may not have come out at the height of the game's popularity, it remains an undeniably fun time, as its confidence and rapid pace make it fly by (no pun intended).

The Angry Birds Movie was a massive box office success, although it was only warmly received critically.

WATCH IT FOR

The vocal performances across the board are fantastic, from Bill Hader to Maya Rudolph, and the animation and faithfulness to the source material are admirable.

SEQUEL?

Yes, the huge success of the first movie led to a sequel, *The Angry Birds Movie 2*, being released in 2019, with Thurop Van Orman directing, and the majority of the cast reprising their roles.

Warcraft

RELEASE DATE
10 June 2016

DIRECTOR
Duncan Jones

STARRING
Travis Fimmel,
Paula Patton,
Dominic Cooper

TAGLINE
"Two Worlds. One
Home."

Warcraft is based on the global phenomenon that should be familiar to anyone with even a passing interest in pop culture. This is mainly due to the success of the massively multiplayer online role-playing game World of Warcraft, which continues to receive expansions and updates to this day, as well as catering to millions of players around the world.

The main Warcraft series began in the early '90s, with the first installment, Warcraft: Orcs & Humans. Developed by Blizzard Entertainment, the real-time strategy game took place in the fantasy world of Azeroth, where fiendish orcs have invaded from another world known as Draenor. Through two campaigns, one focusing on the orcs and the other on the humans of Azeroth, players were tasked with skilfully managing their units in battle, harvesting resources and constructing towns and settlements. Its multiplayer component was praised for its diversity, whereby players could connect locally or through a modem to compete, a relatively new concept at the time of release.

The game was hugely successful, and was followed by two sequels, Warcraft II: Tides of Darkness (1995) and Warcraft III: Reign of Chaos (2002). Both followed the RTS template set by the original, while adding in new elements and improving the graphical fidelity. All games received numerous add-ons and were huge successes. In 2004, the global phenomenon and Warcraft's most famous installment, World of Warcraft, was released. A massively multiplayer online role-playing game, it still gives millions of players around the world access to one of the most robust and evolving fantasy worlds across any medium.

Given the success and rabid fandom of the franchise, adapting Warcraft for film was always going to be a massive undertaking. British director Duncan Jones (director of sci-fi flicks Moon and Source Code, and son of the legendary musician David Bowie – Jareth the Goblin King in

Warcraft: Orcs & Humans – © Blizzard Entertainment

Anduin Lothar (Travis Fimmel) and Garona Halforcen (Paula Patton) – © Universal Pictures

Jim Henson's *Labyrinth*) took on the mammoth task, on top of co-writing the screenplay with Charles Leavitt. Mainly adapting the original game, *Orcs & Humans*, the film also follows the orcs as they leave their world of Draenor to invade Azeroth and its kingdoms.

The movie mainly focuses on Anduin Lothar (Travis Fimmel – *Vikings, Raised By Wolves*), commander of the forces of Stormwind, and Durotan (Toby Kebbell – *RocknRolla, Dawn of the Planet of the Apes*), an orc and the chief of the Frostwolf clan. As in the two campaigns of the original game, the film shows the invasion from contrasting viewpoints, giving the audience real, tangible motives to the orc's actions, rather that painting them as a generic fantasy trope.

"We fight together, or we die together."

– Durotan (Toby Kebbell)

Travis Fimmel is suitably stoic and brave as Lothar, leading with certainty and a steely determination to quell the invasion on his home world. Toby Kebbell gives an emotional performance as Durotan, a family-driven and honourable chieftain who is treated with as much humanity and emotion as any other character. The orcs in *Warcraft* are animated with intimate detail, and are some of the most visually arresting digital characters to be seen on film since the Na'vi in James Cameron's science fiction epic, *Avatar*.

The cast of orcs include Robert Kazinsky *(Pacific Rim, Captain Marvel)*, Clancy Brown (*SpongeBob SquarePants, The Mortuary Collection, Thor: Ragnarok*) and Daniel Wu (*Into the Badlands, Tomb Raider*). Each performer brings something unique to the movie, making the orcs as intriguing, if not more interesting than the majority of the human cast. While audiences may not be on their side, the depth which Duncan Jones gives them ensures they are not just grunts or fodder for infallible heroes.

Durotan (Toby Kebbell) – © Universal Pictures

Warcraft feels otherworldly, and Azeroth looks as though it's covered in a sheen of cleanliness. That's not to say that there is no blood shed in the numerous battles between man and orc, but those who like their fantasy more gritty may not pick up what *Warcraft* is putting down, at least visually. It also falls victim to the tough balance of trying to please two extremely different audiences: those who live and breathe the game world and have encyclopedic knowledge of its lore, and those who are movie-goers looking for an accessible and entertaining fantasy adventure. Game fans may feel that a fraction of the potential of this world was met, especially if they are long-time players of *World of Warcraft* and its multiple expansions. On the other hand, more casual audiences may be lost in the torrent of alien names and the overstuffed cast of characters.

Warcraft had mostly negative reviews, but to date it is the highest-grossing movie based on a video game, showing the franchise's massive draw.

WATCH IT FOR

Toby Kebbell's performance as Durotan is emotional and engrossing, and some of the battles make for colourful and exciting escapism.

SEQUEL?

A new *Warcraft* movie was announced as being in development in late 2020. However, exact details on its status as a sequel or the involvement of any of the original crew, are unknown.

Assassin's Creed

YOUR DESTINY IS IN YOUR BLOOD

ASSASSIN'S CREED

IN THEATERS
DECEMBER 21

RELEASE DATE
21 December 2016

DIRECTOR
Justin Kurzel

STARRING
Michael Fassbender, Marion Cotillard, Jeremy Irons

TAGLINE
"Your Destiny is in Your Blood"

Based on the blockbuster gaming series that began with the eponymous title in 2007, this big-screen adaptation of *Assassin's Creed* is unique in its approach. Rather than loosely adapt a particular game and attempt to translate its story to film, this movie delves into the lore of the games and establishes itself as part of its shared universe. It expands on certain aspects of the series' mythology while trying to remain accessible to general audiences with no knowledge of the games.

Michael Fassbender (*Prometheus, X-Men: First Class, Frank*) plays Callum Lynch, a man whose past is tinged with sadness and whose heart is set on revenge. As he meets his fate on death row, Cal is mysteriously whisked away by Abstergo Industries, a shady entity that researches the past in search of answers. He is hooked up to a machine known as the Animus, which allows him to relive the memories of his ancestors.

> "We work in the dark, to serve the light. We are assassins."
>
> – Callum Lynch (Michael Fassbender)

Aguilar de Nerha (also played by Fassbender) is a devout member of the Brotherhood of Assassins, who spends his time upholding a strict code of honour in his battles against the evil, controlling Templars. The memories play out in the spectacular backdrop of the Spanish Inquisition during the fifteenth century, allowing for mind-bending parkour, rousing swordplay, and a free-fall that was one of the highest undertaken by a stuntman (Damien Walters) in 35 years, at a staggering 125 feet.

The majority of the film, however, takes place in the present day, as Cal learns more about his own past and the hidden abilities inside him. The interior sets of Abstergo are vast, yet clinical. Along with a diverse cast of characters, all with their own strange abilities and links to the past, Cal meets Sophia Rikkin (Marion Cotillard – *Big Fish, A Very Long Engagement, La Vie en Rose*), who

Assassin's Creed – © Ubisoft

Aguilar de Nerha (Michael Fassbender) – © 20th Century Fox

assures him that his journey into his genetic memories is for a greater good, one that will help her and her father find the mysterious 'Apple of Eden' and prevent it from falling into the wrong hands.

The movie had a mixed reception, pleasing some fans of the video games for its faithfulness to the source material, but leaving many movie-goers flummoxed and unsatisfied. Nevertheless,

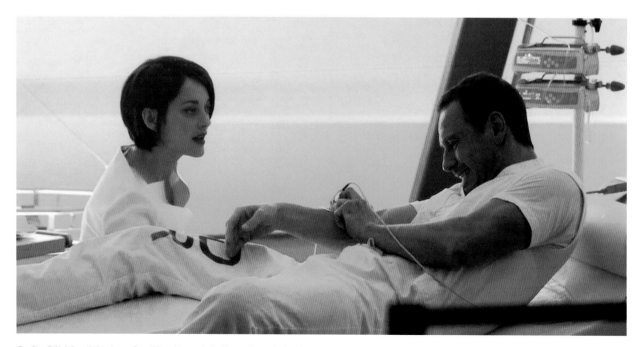

Sofia Rikkin (Marion Cotillard) and Callum Lynch (Michael Fassbender) – © 20th Century Fox

the movie and its events were referenced in the following installment of the video game franchise, *Assassin's Creed Origins* (2017 – PS4, Xbox One, PC), meaning that Cal and Aguilar's adventures remain relevant as the game series continues to rise in popularity.

WATCH IT FOR

The fact that it shares continuity with the games, the colossal Abstergo sets, great combat and parkour and a cameo from the protagonist of *Assassin's Creed Unity* (2014 – PS4, Xbox One, PC), Arno Dorian.

SEQUEL?

Sequels were planned, but were ultimately shelved after Disney acquired the 20th Century Fox studio. However, other adaptations of the franchise have been confirmed, with streaming company Netflix developing a live-action series, an animated series and an anime series.

Resident Evil: The Final Chapter

RELEASE DATE
27 January 2017

DIRECTOR
Paul W.S. Anderson

STARRING
Milla Jovovich, Iain Glen, Ali Larter

TAGLINE
"Evil Comes Home"

Alice's story wrapped up in 2017 with the release of *Resident Evil: The Final Chapter*. After 15 years of steering this action-horror series, video game movie veteran Paul Anderson returned for what would be his fourth and final time in the series. Likewise, Milla Jovovich returned as Alice for one last blast of mutant-crushing mayhem.

After the apocalyptic cliffhanger of *Resident Evil: Retribution*, Alice finds herself wandering a war-torn Washington D.C. in search of survivors and trying her best to stay alive. Facing the remnant undead and other hideous creatures, she soon learns from the artificial intelligence, the Red Queen, that there is an airborne anti-virus that can end the T-virus infection once

Left: Alice (Milla Jovovich) on the run from the undead – © 20th Century Fox

Below: Claire (Ali Larter), Alice (Milla Jovovich) and Abigail (Ruby Rose) – © 20th Century Fox

and for all. In order to obtain it however, she must return to where her nightmare began, the underground research facility known as the Hive.

On Alice's journey she comes across familiar faces as well as all-new characters, both good and bad. Albert Wesker returns as the face of evil for the Umbrella corporation, and Alice is driven by revenge after his devious actions broke her group apart.

> "My name is Alice, and this is my story. The end... of my story."
>
> – Alice (Milla Jovovich)

Like the other films in the franchise, *The Final Chapter* ramps up the action from the get-go. Once its premise is established, the movie is a race against time to end the apocalypse before humanity is lost forever to the inhuman plans of Umbrella. Milla Jovovich is on top form, mixing confidence and vulnerability as Alice refuses to back down while simultaneously carrying the burdens of her origins and her seemingly pointless existence.

Ali Larter returns as Claire Redfield, a more than worthy companion who now knows Alice better than anyone. Newcomers include Ruby Rose (*Orange is the New Black, Batwoman*) as Abigail, a grease monkey who is part of the group that aids Alice in her infiltration of the Hive.

Wrapping up six movies and 15 years worth of storytelling can't be an easy task, but Paul Anderson knows his series inside and out and throws everything at this final installment to make it stick the landing, There's action, nostalgia, sadness, gore, twists and turns aplenty and a rapid pace that makes certain viewers don't get bored. It's not the best *Resident Evil* movie, but it's a solid entry that wraps up the series with a neat little bow.

The movie received mixed reviews, with some praising its action and others lamenting its story and pace. It is the highest-grossing movie in the *Resident Evil* series.

Alice (Milla Jovovich) tries to outrun a winged mutant – © 20th Century Fox

WATCH IT FOR

The neat closure to this blockbuster franchise, a few new beasts and Milla Jovovich giving an emotional and action-packed performance.

SEQUEL?

Unlike other horror franchises that claimed to have a 'final' chapter, this really appears to be the end for the Anderson/Jovovich series. *Resident Evil* returned in November 2021 with a reboot set in Raccoon City in 1998, titled *Resident Evil: Welcome to Raccoon City* and directed by Johannes Roberts (the *47 Metres Down* series, *The Strangers: Prey at Night*).

Alternatively, fans of Capcom's horror series might also be interested in the three computer-generated movies that were produced, set in the same continuity as the games. *Resident Evil: Degeneration* was released in 2008, *Resident Evil: Damnation* in 2012 and, most recently, *Resident Evil: Vendetta* in 2017. All three movies starred series veteran Leon S. Kennedy, as well as some other major characters like Chris Redfield, Claire Redfield and Rebecca Chambers. Netflix also aired a CGI series called *Resident Evil: Infinite Darkness* in 2021. A live-action series is also on the cards.

Tomb Raider

ALICIA VIKANDER IS **LARA CROFT**

TOMB RAIDER

MARCH 16

MGM SQUARE ENIX. GK films EXPERIENCE IT IN **IMAX**

RELEASE DATE
16 March 2018

DIRECTOR
Roar Uthaug

STARRING
Alicia Vikander,
Dominic West,
Walton Goggins

After Core Design's long tenure with the adventure series, developer Crystal Dynamics took up the mantle in 2003, and released a complete reboot in 2013, simply titled *Tomb Raider*. Serving as an origin story for Lara Croft, the game was a much darker and more violent take on the long-running series. It started what would be a new trilogy chronicling Lara's first years as an adventurer, as it was followed by *Rise of the Tomb Raider* (2015) and *Shadow of the Tomb Raider* (2018). Lara's time spent trying to survive, hunt and discover insidious activities while shipwrecked on a mysterious island lent itself perfectly to a cinematic experience, and so work on a new *Tomb Raider* movie, separate from the Angelina Jolie continuity, began in 2017.

Loosely adapting the 2013 game, the film follows Lara as she sets off for the mysterious island of Yamatai, said to have been home to a mythical Queen named Himiko. Lara's father, Richard (Dominic West – *300, John Carter*), had gone missing while investigating Himiko, and so, Lara hires a boat under Captain Lu Ren (Daniel Wu) to locate the island. Once there, they find themselves at the mercy of Trinity, an organisation looking to harness Himiko's power for presumably nefarious means. Mathias Vogel (Walton Goggins – *Django Unchained, The Shield*) leads the expedition, and he takes Lara and Ren prisoner. What follows is a breathless adventure across Yamatai in a race to uncover its dark secrets and learn about Richard Croft's fate.

Like the video game's history, this reboot sets a completely different tone from the duology of Angelina Jolie-led pictures. Whereas those films leaned on Lara's confidence and her physical training, this newer version brings Lara's youth and naivety to the forefront, although Alicia Vikander takes her on a character arc full of physical and emotional growth. Her search for her father and discovery of his fate lends a gravity to her actions, and the juxtaposition between her flippant life on the mainland and the life-or-death situations she finds herself in on Yamatai shows the young adventurer's rapid maturity.

Tomb Raider – © Square Enix

Lu Ren (Daniel Wu) and Lara Croft (Alicia Vikander) – © Warner Bros. Pictures

Mathias Vogel (Walton Goggins) – © Warner Bros. Pictures

"I need you."

– Lara Croft (Alicia Vikander)

"No, you don't. You are worth ten of me."

– Richard Croft (Dominic West)

The action in this movie is exhilarating at times, and much more grounded in realism than the more fantastical acrobatics of the previous two movies. Lu Ren and Lara are forces to be reckoned with as they traverse the jungle to defeat Vogel's men. While only loosely adapting the 2013 reboot game, the movie manages to retain some of its gritty tone, while not venturing into quite as dark a territory as the source material.

Fans of the more recent titles in the *Tomb Raider* series should feel comfortable giving this film a shot. It's not going to set the world on fire, but Vikander's performance along with Roar Uthaug's solid direction of the action means this adaptation is in as good hands as fans could realistically hope for.

Tomb Raider is one of the more well-received video game adaptations, with critics praising Alicia Vikander's performance and the well-rounded and entertaining action scenes. It was a box office success.

WATCH IT FOR

A fresh new take on Lara Croft, the mysterious setting and the satisfying and exciting shoot-outs.

SEQUEL?

A sequel is currently in production, with up-and-coming director Misha Green signed on to write and direct.

Rampage

RELEASE DATE
13 April 2018

DIRECTOR
Brad Peyton

STARRING
Dwayne Johnson,
Naomie Harris,
Jeffrey Dean
Morgan

TAGLINE
"Big Meets
Bigger"

© Warner Bros. Pictures

*R*ampage was a unique and destructive arcade experience first released in 1986. Up to three players could control massive, kaiju-style monsters as they tried to reduce a series of buildings to rubble. The chaotic gameplay and endearing, if wholly evil characters coupled with a cartoon style made the game appeal to both arcade and home console players. Its success ensured the series saw multiple sequels throughout the '90s and 2000s, with the three creatures moving from the United States setting of the original to global destruction across multiple continents. They even ended up travelling through time on their relentless rampage.

The addictive and comical adventures of George (a giant gorilla), Lizzie (a gargantuan lizard creature) and Ralph (a vicious, massive wolf) inspired Hollywood to get the ball rolling on a movie adaptation of this unique series.

A more substantial and relatable storyline was needed in order to draw people in. Casting Dwayne Johnson in the lead role as Davis Okoye was a sure-fire way to ensure that the film would draw in a casual movie-going audience, and the monstrous destruction on show in the movie provides enough visual spectacle to satisfy action and monster movie fans.

At the heart of the movie is George and Davis' relationship. Knowing in his heart that George does not have an inherently destructive nature, Davis defends his simian friend to the very end.

Left: *Rampage: World Tour* –
© Warner Bros. Interactive
Entertainment

Below: George and Davis Okoye
(Dwayne Johnson) –
© Warner Bros. Pictures

Davis (Dwayne Johnson) and Ralph – © Warner Bros. Pictures

Dwayne Johnson give a genuinely heart-felt performance in this movie, and the special effects on show as regards the three colossal, mutated beasts ensure the movie is a feast for the eyes.

> "How about you take these cuffs off and find out yourself, brother?"
> – Davis Okoye (Dwayne Johnson)

The rivalry between Davis and the villainous Harvey Russell (Jeffrey Dean Morgan – *The Walking Dead, Supernatural, Watchmen*) makes for some amusing and tension-filled scenes. As regards the nature of film versus game, clearly a more serious tone was developed for the adaptation, as the video game's over-the-top cartoon style was replaced. That's not to say there's nothing inherently outlandish in the events being depicted, but director Brad Peyton treads an admirable line between an action spectacle and a cheesy, charming adventure.

Rampage was a huge box office success and was one of the more well-received video game movies.

WATCH IT FOR

The spectacle of the destructive creatures, the stand-off moments with Davis and Harvey, and George's bond with Davis.

SEQUEL?

No official announcement has been made regarding a sequel.

Dead Trigger

RELEASE DATE
3 May 2019

DIRECTOR
Mike Cuff & Scott Windhauser

STARRING
Dolph Lundgren, Autumn Reeser, Romeo Miller

© Saban Films

*D*ead Trigger (2012) is a hit zombie-killing app: a first person, mission-based arcade-style game which pits players against hordes of the undead while they complete tasks like area traversal and location defence. The original game was followed by a sequel, *Dead Trigger 2* (2013), and obviously going on the big and small screen's insatiable appetite for zombie-based media, a movie version was put into production.

The film stars action legend Dolph Lundgren (*Rocky IV, Masters of the Universe, the Expendables* series) as Captain Kyle Walker, a grizzled zombie-killing veteran. He leads a team of recruits known as Dead Triggers: young adults who were enlisted from a gaming programme designed to locate people with proficiency in combat against the infected. The new team is tasked with locating a group of scientists who might have discovered a cure for the rampant virus.

Like 2003's *House of the Dead, Dead Trigger* makes no bones about what it is: a shlocky, blood-filled B-movie. Most of the young cast are unknowns and some of them turn out to be fairly endearing. The movie has plenty of zombie-killing action, but it inexplicably feels pretty muted, despite the special effects being quite decent for the budget. It sometimes slows to a crawl for no real reason, underplaying both the severity of the threat and the importance of the mission.

Likewise, the group often appear completely non-plussed about their battles with the undead. This may be intentional so as to show how jaded they are due to the length of the outbreak, but it's hard to comprehend how anyone could be so casual about the life-or-death situations they find themselves in.

"Alright Dead Triggers, show me what you can do."

– Kyle Walker (Dolph Lundgren)

Dead Trigger – © Madfinger Games

Left: Kyle Walker (Dolph Lundgren) –
© Saban Films

Below: Tara (Autumn Reeser), Kyle (Dolph Lundgren) and Chris (Chris Galya) – © Saban Films

Lundgren is the saviour of the film, and Walker is a genuinely likeable character. Not stereotypically dismissive or a loose cannon, he respects the recruits and works with them to teach and protect them. As their mission continues and their numbers dwindle, he remains a reliable leader, despite having his own personal struggles to deal with.

Dead Trigger won't turn any heads or set the genre on fire, but it's a harmless, if somewhat bland entry into the zombie-flooded market. It wasn't received well critically.

WATCH IT FOR

Dolph Lundgren's Kyle Walker, who's an enjoyable lead and some popcorn, throwaway zombie action.

SEQUEL?

There has been no news or movement towards a *Dead Trigger* sequel.

Pokémon – Detective Pikachu

RELEASE DATE
10 May 2019

DIRECTOR
Rob Letterman

STARRING
Justice Smith,
Ryan Reynolds,
Kathryn Newton

With the *Pokémon* series only going from strength to strength with each release, and the highly successful anime series and long running animated film series consistently releasing new installments, it made sense to finally bring *Pokémon* into live action. Given the popularity of the instantly recognisable mascot, Pikachu, producers decided to adapt the Nintendo 3DS game, *Detective Pikachu*, for a Hollywood outing.

Directed by Rob Letterman and loosely following the plot of the game, it introduces Tim (Justice Smith - *Jurassic World: Fallen Kingdom, The Get Down*), an insurance agent who lost his father, a police detective, in an unfortunate accident. When he comes across a talking Pikachu (Ryan Reynolds) who claims to have been his father's Pokémon, the two don their investigating hats (one figuratively, one literally) to try and solve the case regarding Tim's dad and the accident which caused his disappearance.

Detective Pikachu had a large task set out before it. After more than 20 animated movies about the pocket monsters and their vast world, and plenty of series of the anime to boot, putting this world and these beloved creatures onto the big screen, in live action, was surely no small task.

Thankfully, *Pokémon* fans could rest easy once the movie was released. Set in Ryme City, where people and Pokémon co-exist, the film is a veritable showcase for the franchise and the 800 species of Pokémon to be found within.

From Pikachu to Charizard to Mister Mime and Psyduck, the creatures are meticulously animated and given an uncanny, textured look. It never really feels like Tim and Lucy (Kathryn Newton – *Big Little Lies, Supernatural*) are conversing with unconvincing CGI monstrosities, but real, living creatures, and it goes a long way to giving the movie the authenticity it needs to be a success.

There are laughs aplenty thanks to fantastic performances from Ryan Reynolds and Justice Smith, and the movie is filled with Pokémon-battling action and several interesting, and sometimes heartfelt, twists. The direction and script-writing manages a perfect balance,

Tim and Detective Pikachu in *Detective Pikachu* for Nintendo 3DS – © The Pokémon Company

Tim (Justice Smith), Detective Pikachu (Ryan Reynolds) and Lucy (Kathryn Newton) – © Warner Bros. Pictures

Charizard and Detective Pikachu mid-battle – © Warner Bros. Pictures

ensuring there is enough fan-service to please die-hard gamers, enough silliness to keep younger audience members happy and enough accessibility to keep casual movie-goers and adults entertained throughout.

"That's a twist. That's very twisty..."
– Detective Pikachu (Ryan Reynolds)

Pokémon – Detective Pikachu was a huge hit financially and got mostly positive reviews from critics.

WATCH IT FOR

The authentic design of each creature, the exciting and unpredictable story, and the endearing and hilarious performances from cast.

SEQUEL?

Unsurprisingly, a sequel is in development, with Oren Uziel signed on as screenwriter.

The Angry Birds Movie 2

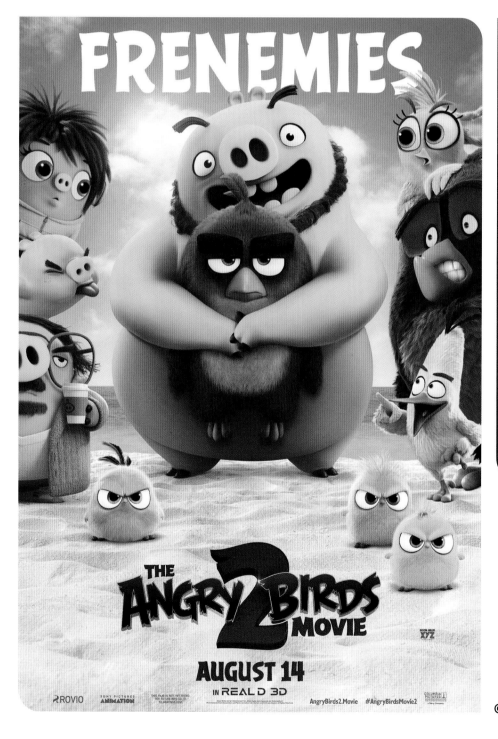

© Sony Pictures Releasing

RELEASE DATE
14 August 2019

DIRECTOR
Thurop Van Orman

STARRING THE VOICES OF
Jason Sudeikis, Leslie Jones, Josh Gad

TAGLINE
"Frenemies"

The world-famous birds and piggies return for another round of colourful hijinks. This time around, the "frenemies" must reluctantly unite towards a common goal. Zeta (Leslie Jones – *Ghostbusters*, *Saturday Night Live*) from Eagle Island, is looking to claim the other two islands for herself, as she suffers under the frozen conditions of her own dwelling. The birds and the piggies set about infiltrating Eagle Island to put a stop to Zeta's destructive ice cannon.

The Mighty Eagle is nervous about the confrontation, as his past with Zeta threatens to catch up with him. The reluctant heroes nevertheless try a number of increasingly ludicrous plans to try to gain access to Zeta's fortress unnoticed.

The laughs come thick and fast in this animated sequel, largely owed to the fantastic animation and vocal performances. Leslie Jones makes for a likeable and ridiculous villain, and her past with Peter Dinklage's cowardly Mighty Eagle make for some cringey and hilarious scenes.

The film is successful in that difficult task; trying to keep both children and adults entertained for the duration. Thanks to its speedy pace, hyperactive characters and witty one-liners, *The Angry Birds Movie 2* is another hoot (!) for this comedy series.

> "Time for Plan X."
>
> – Silver (Rachel Bloom)

> "Plan X?? I thought you said Spandex!!"
>
> – Leonard (Bill Hader)

The Angry Birds Movie 2 was a success with critics and a hit at the box office. At the time of release, it was the highest-rated movie based on a video game.

Angry Birds 2 – © Rovio

Above: **The cast of** *The Angry Birds* *Movie 2* **– © Sony Pictures Releasing**

Right: **Zeta (Leslie Jones) – © Sony Pictures Releasing**

WATCH IT FOR

Red and Leonard's back-and-forths, with Red being as sarcastically condescending as ever, the icy new villain, Zeta, and the scene in which the heroes try to dress up as an eagle to gain access to Zeta's lair.

SEQUEL?

No announcement has been made as regards a sequel, but it stands to reason that the birds and piggies will return in some form,

The Best of the Rest – 2010s

Throughout the decade, several high-profile games made their way to the small screen in the form of TV movies, direct-to-video or streaming titles.

Xbox's flagship series, the sci-fi military shooter *Halo*, was given screen treatment with the tie-in *Halo 4: Forward Unto Dawn*, which acted as a prequel to *Halo 4*. The fourth mainline entry was released in November 2012 for the Xbox 360, and later in 2014 for Xbox One.

Forward Unto Dawn came a month earlier, initially as a web series before being edited into a feature-length film. The film was praised for its mix of quality computer-generated effects and live action and for its portrayal of series protagonist, Master Chief.

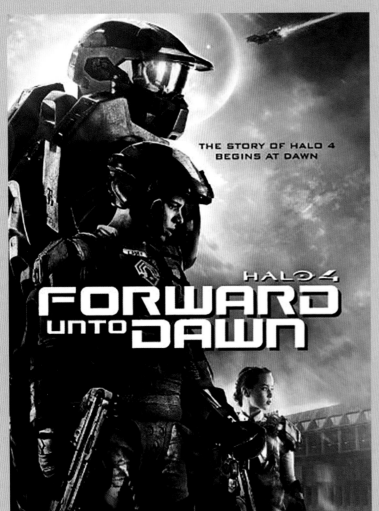

THE STORY OF HALO 4
BEGINS AT DAWN

HALO 4
FORWARD UNTO DAWN

The hack-and-slash action game *Dante's Inferno* was adapted into a gothic animation called *Dante's Inferno: An Animated Epic*.

A highly-acclaimed adaptation of the *Phoenix Wright* courtroom drama series, entitled *Ace Attorney*, was released in 2012, capturing the frantic and amusing drama of the popular games.

An animated film set during the events of the mammoth sci-fi game *Mass Effect 2*, entitled *Mass Effect: Paragon Lost*, was released in 2012. Bungie and 343's *Halo* was represented not only with *Forward Unto Dawn*, but with no less than seven short films, collectively known as *Halo Legends*.

Halo 4: Forward Unto Dawn –
© 343 Industries

Ace Attorney – © Toho

Indie Game: The Movie arrived in 2012, from Canadian filmmakers Lisanne Pajot and James Swirsky. It features in-depth interviews with the creators of some of the most prominent independent video game releases in history, including *Fez, Braid* and *Super Meat Boy*. The emphasis is on the emotional effort and struggles that go hand-in-hand with developing your own vision without major studio support. It was well received by most corners of the gaming and film communities.

Platinum Games' fluid and violent action series *Bayonetta* received an anime movie in 2013. An adaptation of the first game and following the Umbran witch in a battle between angels and demons, it was entitled *Bayonetta: Bloody Fate*.

Throughout the 2010s, several animated movies based on the popular, spook-filled RPG *Yo-kai Watch* were released, as well as movies based on Atlus' hugely popular *Persona* RPG series.

Batman: Assault on Arkham was released in 2014, and is set in the *Arkham* universe of video games (*Arkham Asylum, Arkham City, Arkham Origins* and *Arkham Knight)*.

A movie animated in the same style as the sword-based action game *Heavenly Sword* was also released in 2014.

Capcom's more light-hearted alternative to *Resident Evil*, the *Dead Rising* series, was brought to the medium with two TV movies, *Dead Rising: Watchtower* (2015) and *Dead Rising: Endgame* (2016), both starring Jesse Metcalfe (*Desperate Housewives, John Tucker Must Die*) as zombie-killing hero Chase Carter.

2015 also saw the release of *Pixels*, a family film with a video game-themed storyline and a plethora of appearances by well-known characters, most prominently Namco's fruit devouring, yellow hero, Pac-man.

The two *Jumanji* sequels, *Jumanji: Welcome to the Jungle* (2017) and *Jumanji: The Next Level* (2019) both replaced the original film's board game premise with a video game that sucks players inside, giving them avatars with special skills and radically different appearances than their real-world counterparts.

Steven Spielberg directed a film adaptation of the massively popular novel, *Ready Player One* (2018), which contains a video game-heavy storyline concerning a virtual world called OASIS. A golden 'easter egg' hidden within promises full ownership of the system to whoever finds it. The movie is filled with pop culture references, from *A Nightmare on Elm Street* and *The Shining* to *Voltron, Jurassic Park* and even *Last Action Hero*.

Sonic the Hedgehog

RELEASE DATE
14 February 2020

DIRECTOR
Jeff Fowler

STARRING
James Marsden,
Ben Schwartz, Jim
Carrey

TAGLINE
"When the World
Needs a Hero...
Think Fast"

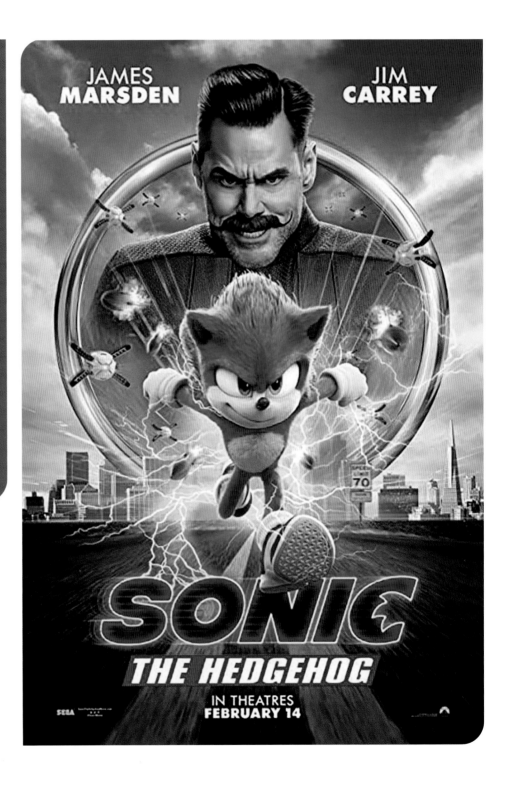

Like the immensely popular *Super Mario* series, *Sonic the Hedgehog* garnered its own massive fanbase with a series of well-received, fast-paced platformers, beginning on SEGA's 16-bit console and continuing in various forms to this day. A movie adaptation of the 'blue blur' had been gestating since the '90s, a decade which saw Nintendo's *Super Nintendo Entertainment System* and SEGA's *Mega Drive/Genesis* do battle for gamers' hearts and cash in the now infamous 'Console Wars'. While Nintendo's portly plumber got his chance with the sci-fi extravaganza *Super Mario Bros.* in 1993, it would be over two decades later when fans would finally see the famous hedgehog make the leap to the big screen.

In 2019, SEGA and Paramount Pictures revealed a teaser poster for their upcoming *Sonic* adaptation, and it caused a lot of buzz... for mostly the wrong reasons. Fans were perplexed at Sonic's odd, human-like proportions, but many seemed content and cautiously optimistic to wait to see the character in motion before casting a stone. When the first trailer for the movie was revealed in April 2019, it was met with widespread criticism. Fans lamented the design of the character for being far removed from the iconic look of the video game series, with Sonic having no gloves, small eyes and 'terrifyingly human' teeth.

> "With great power comes great, power-hungry bad guys!"
>
> – Sonic (Ben Schwartz)

So massive was the backlash, that the studio decided to go back to drawing board and re-work the character to be more in line with the familiar design that video game fans loved. The film was pushed back by three months to February 2020 in order to give the animators 'a little more time to make Sonic just right'. (Jeff Fowler, Director)

The film sees Sonic (voiced by Ben Schwartz – *Parks and Recreation, House of Lies*) transported from his world to Green Hills, Montana, where he teams up with police officer Tom Wachowski (James Marsden – *The Notebook,* the *X-Men* series), who reluctantly agrees to help him locate his magic rings while evading capture at the hands of the evil Dr. Robotnik (Jim Carrey – *The Mask,* the *Ace Ventura* series, *Batman Forever*).

There is care and fun aplenty to be found in *Sonic the Hedgehog*, with a mix of family-friendly fun, multiple nods to the games (including the famous 'SEEEEGGGAAAA' jingle that greeted gamers in the Mega Drive/Genesis games) and great chemistry between the cast members. For a series that began in the 1990s, it's fitting to have comedic icon Jim Carrey present here, and the back-and-forths between his Robotnik and James Marsden's Tom Wachowski make for some genuinely funny moments, meaning there is something for all ages in this adaptation.

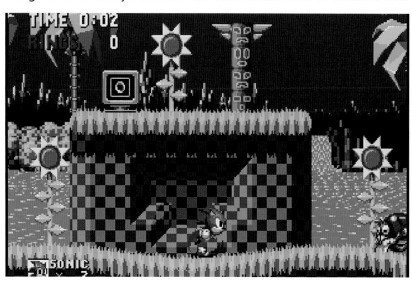

Sonic the Hedgehog – © SEGA

Above: Sonic (Ben Schwartz) and Tom (James Marsden) – © Paramount Pictures

Left: Dr. Robotnik (Jim Carrey) – © Paramount Pictures

WATCH IT FOR

The easter eggs for game fans, Jim Carrey and James Marsden's comedic scenes and the mid-credits scene.

SEQUEL?

Yes, a sequel has been confirmed, with a release date of 8 April 2022. The same directing and writing team will reprise their duties.

Monster Hunter

© Sony Pictures Releasing

RELEASE DATE
18 December 2020

DIRECTOR
Paul W.S. Anderson

STARRING
Milla Jovovich, Tony Jaa, Ron Perlman

Capcom's intricate action-RPG franchise has become as colossal as the beasts that inhabit it. The *Monster Hunter* series began on the PlayStation 2 and has only gone from strength to strength as it released sequels and enhanced updates, finding particular success on handheld systems such as the PlayStation Portable and the Nintendo 3DS.

Each iteration of the series has you taking on the role of a hunter, whose job it is to track and either destroy or capture gigantic and powerful monsters, from hulking, dinosaur-like lizards to fabulously feathered beasts. Each monster requires a different tactic to break its defence and inflict damage, and battles can take upwards of 40 minutes to complete, whether solo or in local or online multiplayer, depending on the version. You can do so with a myriad of weapon types, from lances to bows to ridiculously over-sized swords. After a monster is slain, players can strip various hides, scales and other materials from the beasts to enhance armour and weapons.

In 2018, the series released its fifth mainline installment, *Monster Hunter: World* (PS4, Xbox One, PC). The core gameplay remained similar to the successful past entries, but the in-game world had been opened up by the power of the newer console generation. The game allows for seamless travel between areas where they were once sectioned off to process the loading times associated with such massive games. Now, in the New World, the plant and animal life is more active, the monsters interact and fight in a more dynamic way than before, and traversal has been streamlined to give the game more fluidity than ever before.

This continued in the next release, *Monster Hunter: Rise* (2021 – Nintendo Switch), and the game contains those same quality of life changes along with a greater focus on the verticality of the world.

Monster Hunter: World was critically acclaimed and is, to date, Capcom's single best-selling release. Inspired by the overwhelming success, the movie rights were handed over to none other than video game movie veteran, Paul W.S. Anderson. He cast his wife, Milla Jovovich, in the lead role, and set about making a movie that would entertain newcomers and satiate die-hard fans of the game series.

Monster Hunter goes full Hollywood right out of the gate, following a group of soldiers in the desert on a rescue mission. The close-knit, wise-cracking team are led by Captain Natalie Artemis (Milla Jovovich). When they're caught in the middle of a massive storm, they find

Monster Hunter: World – © Capcom

themselves whisked away to an unknown world, where they're confronted with dangerous beasts unlike anything they've ever encountered before.

"Choc-o-late!!"

– the Hunter (Tony Jaa)

The first act of the movie is part-adventure, part-nightmare. The game series has always blended epic battles with eclectic, off-the-wall whimsy and comical elements, to great effect. That personality is completely absent for the first act of the movie, which sees the team get assaulted by terrifying creatures in an underground cave system. The games have sparingly used blood during certain attacks, and the player character only ever really faints or is otherwise inoffensively dispatched by the creatures. The movie, however, has some bizarre violence and gore in this act that feels totally out of place.

Things start to feel more like the game when Artemis comes across the Hunter (Tony Jaa – the *Ong-Bak* trilogy, the *Warrior King* series), from whom she begins to learn about this mysterious New World, the creatures that inhabit it, and how she can possibly return home.

There are some enjoyable exchanges between Jovovich and Jaa, miscommunications that lead to comical moments. The majority of the run time is spent with these two characters, which might be an enjoyable prospect for those who are looking for a grand, isolated adventure in the wilderness. That enjoyment also hinges on the chemistry between these two characters, so the pace might not suit audience members looking for all-out action.

There are amusing elements from the game that remain intact. The monster design of the dreaded Diablos and the mighty Rathalos are fairly spot-on, and the weapons and acrobatics on show should please game purists. Likewise, the inclusion of the Hunter cooking meat on a spit (a common activity in the games) and the appearance of the feline -

Rathalos – © Sony Pictures Releasing

Captain Natalie Artemis (Milla Jovovich) and the Hunter (Tony Jaa) – © Sony Pictures Releasing

or Felyne in the Monster Hunter universe - Palicoes, in the form of Meowscular Chef (a cat... that cooks), ensure there is enough for game fans to be happy with.

Monster Hunter feels more like the start of a franchise than a fully-fledged movie, but it seems unlikely this series will be as well received as the games it's based on.

WATCH IT FOR

Artemis and the Hunter's comradery, the awesome creature design and game characters like Handler, Admiral and Meowscular Chef.

SEQUEL?

Unknown. Time will tell if this movie is enough of a hit to warrant a return to the New World.

Mortal Kombat

RELEASE DATE
23 April 2021

DIRECTOR
Simon McQuoid

STARRING
Lewis Tan,
Hiroyuki Sanada,
Jessica McNamee

TAGLINE
"GET OVER
HERE!"

While slightly revitalised on the small screen with the short film *Mortal Kombat: Rebirth* and the web series, *Mortal Kombat: Legacy*, the hyper-violent fantasy fighting series had been dormant in cinemas for nearly 25 years.

The resurgence in popularity for the gaming series hasn't waned, with the newer reboot-through-time travel installments faring well with fans and critics alike. *Mortal Kombat* (2011), *Mortal Kombat X* (2015) and *Mortal Kombat 11* (2019) all seemed to scratch that itch for fantasy fighting fans and made the series successful and relevant in the modern landscape.

A new iteration of the movie series was brought to the table by director Simon McQuoid, and it was his directorial debut for film. Like the two previous films, it focuses on the inter-dimensional tournament, Mortal Kombat, and the battle between Earthrealm and Outworld, presided over by the malevolent sorcerer Shang Tsung (Chin Han – *The Dark Knight, Contagion*). While it brings many fan favourites to the table, such as Liu Kang, Kano, Raiden, Scorpion, Sonya and Sub-Zero, the main protagonist this time around is an original character, Cole Young, played by Lewis Tan (*Deadpool 2, Iron Fist*).

Cole is an amateur cage fighter who is whisked towards an uncertain destiny owed to a dragon mark he has beared since birth. A chosen fighter, he allies himself with Earthrealm's warriors to stop Shang Tsung from ending the tournament before it can even begin.

There's no doubting *Mortal Kombat*'s reverence for its source material. The whole movie is rife with the dark, gothic atmosphere that makes the games so appealing. There are plenty of references to the series throughout, both to the ever-expanding deep lore and amusing meta jokes on the fighting genre in general. One particular instance has Liu Kang continually using the same move to secure a victory during training, a clear riff on the much-maligned button mashers so prevalent in complex fighting games. Likewise, the foul-mouthed Kano (Josh Lawson – *House of Lies, Anchorman 2: The Legend Continues*) is consistently unimpressed with his serious and mystical comrades, ridiculing their ways and becoming increasingly frustrated at his inability to unlock his 'arcana', a sort of special move or magical power that

Liu Kang (Ludi Lin) and Kung Lao (Max Huang) – © Warner Bros. Pictures

Mileena (Sisi Stringer) – © Warner Bros. Pictures

every champion has within them. Kano's interactions with the cast are an absolute highlight of the movie, and it's tough to remember a comic relief character that's been as effective in recent years.

A big part of the marketing for the film centred around the characters of Scorpion and Sub-Zero, and it's easy to see why. The rivalry between these two is the core of the film, and the tragic opening scene sets the stage for an epic revenge tale from beyond the grave. Die-hard fans should be happy at the portrayal of these iconic characters, both in their signature fantastical fighting styles and their emotional portrayals by Hiroyuki Sanada (Scorpion) and Joe Taslim (Sub-Zero). Taslim brings an imposing dominance to the character, akin to a slasher arriving as a one-man army to try and eliminate as many of Earthrealm's champions as possible.

> "Do not forget this face."
> – Hanzo Hasashi (Scorpion – Hiroyuki Sanada)

Then, there are the fights themselves. The choreography on show is fantastic, and it's framed wonderfully by Simon McQuoid's stylish direction. Adrenaline-pumping martial arts are set against a mixture of fantasy and realism, as battles take place across Earthrealm and Outworld. The rigidity of the tournament is absent, and so the film thunders on in its final act, as a plan is hatched and several high-profile fights take place simultaneously. The talking point of these is, naturally, the 'fatalities'. These ultra-gory finishing moves from the video game series are finally given full-blown live-action treatment, and they do not disappoint. Not for the squeamish, the blood, guts and gore fly liberally as characters are decimated in inventive and gruesome ways. The filmmakers pull no punches and no one is safe as the realms battle for their ultimate destinies.

Scorpion (Hiroyuki Sanada) – © Warner Bros. Pictures

Mortal Kombat is a different beast from the two films that came before it. It's still rich in the franchise's history, and a great chunk of characters make their appearance, including the leader and Thunder God, Lord Raiden (Tadanobu Asano – *47 Ronin, Thor:Ragnarok*). The story flies by at a breakneck pace, the dialogue can be a little hammy at times, and the final act is deceptive in how quickly things are wrapped up. Ultimately, this movie should please many fans of the previous movies and the game series, but it very much feels like the first step for a franchise with great ambitions for the future. And, most importantly, the Techno Syndrome theme from the original movies is present and accounted for in remix form. TEST YOUR MIGHT!!

The film was a box office success but received mixed reviews from critics.

WATCH IT FOR

The choreography and brutal fatalities, genuinely interesting characterisations and cast of recognisable series staples, and the memorable, scene-stealing performance by Josh Lawson as Kano.

SEQUEL?

It seems likely that this iteration of *Mortal Kombat* will continue, as Sub-Zero actor Joe Taslim has signed a contract for four more movies.

Dynasty Warriors

RELEASE DATE
29 April 2021

DIRECTOR
Roy Chow

STARRING
Wang Kai, Louis Koo, Han Geng

Developers KOEI followed their tactical conquest series, *Romance of the Three Kingdoms,* with a more action-orientated offshoot called *Dynasty Warriors.* The first game in the series was a one-on-one fighter, similar to *Street Fighter* and other games of that type. However, *Dynasty Warriors 2*, which was actually a spin-off in Japan and not a main installment, began the gameplay loop that fans of the series have become so familiar with. Players take control of a number of Chinese warriors in battlefields that span regions of China during the rule of the Han Dynasty, and as such, get to play on differing sides of a conflict that is filled with twists and turns, as well as over-the-top, stylish action.

Players are typically faced with dozens of enemies that they can plough through with a multitude of weapons including swords, spears, maces and bows. As enemies are picked off, a gauge is filled with 'Musou', an energy that allows players to unleash show-stopping magical attacks that eliminate whole groups of enemies. The games offer fantastical retellings of some of the major conflicts told in the old *Three Kingdoms* texts and the *Romance of the Three Kingdoms* novel. The series is now nine major entries in, with dozens of spin-offs and expanded versions in the form of the *Empires* and *Xtreme Legends* versions. *Samurai Warriors* is a sister series that instead moves the action to feudal Japan, and *Warriors Orochi* brings the characters of *Dynasty Warriors* and *Samurai Warriors* together in a fantasy mash-up. The iconic brand of *Warriors* gameplay has been expanded to other properties, namely Nintendo's *The Legend of Zelda* series, with the action-packed *Hyrule Warriors* series, and the tactical role-playing series *Fire Emblem,* with *Fire Emblem Warriors.* The revered Japanese RPG series *Persona* also used the engine for the action game *Persona 5 Strikers* (2020 – PS4, PC, Nintendo Switch).

The film version of *Dynasty Warriors* was directed by Roy Chow, and mostly adheres to the tales of the Three Kingdoms as fans know them. Featuring over-the-top battles (and outfits), aerial nature shots galore and about six strategic planning scenes too many, it encompasses the video games and the lore of ancient China in one grand, sweeping epic. Following the usurping of the throne by the malicious and slovenly Dong Zhuo (Lam Suet), three warriors attempt to end his reign by gathering a force large and powerful enough to defeat the unhinged Lü Bu (Louis Koo), Dong Zhuo's seemingly unbeatable general. Liu Bei (Tony Yang), Zhang Fei

Dynasty Warriors 9 –
© **KOEI**

Liu Bei (Tony Yang) in battle – © Newport Entertainment

(Justin Cheung) and Guan Yu (Han Geng) join forces with the brave Cao Cao (Wang Kai) in order to foster enough strength to overthrow the false leader and reclaim the land. They're aided by the acquisition of mystical weapons that can help them turn the tide against the forces of Lü Bu, leading to the ridiculous action fans of the video games know and love.

Swathes of soldiers are thrown about like rag dolls as the warriors execute cartoonish and satisfying attacks, defying gravity and logic as they cut through their enemies' ranks. Coupled with the same solo-filled rock and metal soundtrack as the game series, the battles should satisfy fans, at least on a surface level. While the story in the games is mostly brief and dramatic, here there are extended periods of slow world building, gentle romantic moments and political intrigue. These scenes can be offset by how ludicrous the movie becomes, but as long as you have any familiarity with the source, it should be easy to go along for the ride. In contrast, prior knowledge definitely helps, as some scenes can zip by with little explanation and hastily introduced characters, meaning viewers could be excused for drifting away from the plot and enjoying the visuals alone.

"A swallow cannot fathom an eagle's dream."

– Cao Cao (Wang Kai)

Dynasty Warriors makes no excuse for what it is: an action-epic, framed against a real history of China but oftentimes jazzed up beyond recognition. It's *Crouching Tiger Hidden Dragon* turned up to 1,000, and if it's on-screen chaos you crave, these two hours could very well deliver.

Dong Zhuo (Lam Suet) sits atop his throne – © Newport Entertainment

WATCH IT FOR

The brilliant casting, authentic soundtrack and fantastical battle scenes.

SEQUEL?

While no sequel is on the cards, the movie has an extremely open-ended finale, meaning there could well be more adventures for the empowered warriors.

Werewolves Within

RELEASE DATE
25 June 2021

DIRECTOR
Josh Ruben

STARRING
Sam Richardson,
Milana Vayntrub,
Wayne Duvall

TAGLINE
"A Whodunnit
With Teeth"

Werewolves Within brought an inspired, socially-orientated virtual reality experience to devices in 2016. Available for PlayStation VR, HTC Vive and Oculus Rift, the game sees players sitting around a crystal ball in a fantasy town that has become victim to werewolf attacks. Players are assigned roles, and a number of them are secretly werewolves. Through voice chat, players try to deduce who is lying and is in fact, a deadly invader. You can check through a notebook at any time to keep track of each player and their assigned roles to see if their story checks out. The stylised characters are emotive and well designed, and there is riotous fun to be had in deceiving and deducing, either with friends or strangers.

The movie adaptation was announced in 2018, with game developer Ubisoft producing through Ubisoft Motion Pictures. Josh Ruben was approached by the company for directorial duties after they were impressed with his horror-comedy *Scare Me* (2020). When ranger Finn Wheeler (Sam Richardson) is assigned to Beaverfield, a small town undergoing a huge change in the form of a proposed pipeline, he comes across the town's quirky residents. Cecily (Milana Vayntrub), the local post-lady, is his guide to small-town gossip, and the two become friendly as Finn tries to settle into his new post. When a blizzard cuts off the power to the town, the residents take refuge in a nearby lodge, and things soon begin to go bump in the night.

Werewolves Within is a deft blend of horror and comedy, never taking itself too seriously but still delivering on some genuine thrills. The comedy feels natural and unintrusive, and while the characters are larger than life, they still feel grounded in reality thanks to stellar dialogue and biting sarcasm. Paranoia abounds as the violence and bizarre goings-on ramp up, with the residents beginning to question if there's an animalistic monster among them, picking them off and turning them against one another. The movie keeps the audience guessing, building a perfect pace towards the finale. The two leads are genuinely likeable and their chemistry

Werewolves Within – © Ubisoft

The cast of *Werewolves Within* – © IFC Films

is natural. Sam Richardson in particular, is one of the most well-written and relatable main characters in a video game movie, with his patience and commitment to protecting the band of misfits leading to some heart-warming moments.

With a gripping story, fantastic acting and direction and special effects that only add to the story rather than overload it, *Werewolves Within* is a fantastic movie in its own right, even if

Emerson Flint (Glenn Fleshler) in *Werewolves Within* – © IFC Films

you have no familiarity with the game it's based on, or video games in general. It eschews the fantasy setting for a modern take, but still gives audiences laughs, shocks and head-scratching twists.

"This town's bats*%t."

– Cecily Moore (Milana Vayntrub)

It was very well received by critics and, at the time of writing, is the most critically-acclaimed movie based on a video game, surpassing *The Angry Birds Movie 2.*

WATCH IT FOR

The intriguing and twisting mystery, the subtle and genuinely funny comedic moments and great acting from a fantastic ensemble cast.

SEQUEL?

At the time of writing, no sequel has been announced, but it's possible given its critical reception.

The Future...

Regardless of the hit-and-miss nature of adaptations over the last thirty years, Hollywood's fascination with video games shows no signs of slowing down. 2021 saw the release of more major adaptations in Simon McQuoid's new *Mortal Kombat* reboot, the action-packed *Dynasty Warriors*, the horror-comedy *Werewolves Within* and *Resident Evil: Welcome to Raccoon City*.

In 2022, adventurer Nathan Drake leaps to live action in a big-screen prequel version of *Uncharted*, with Tom Holland (*Spider-Man: Homecoming*) as a young Drake, and Mark Wahlberg as his mentor, Victor 'Sully' Sullivan.

Sonic the Hedgehog 2 arrives in 2022, and a seemingly never-ending slate of game adaptations will follow.

The indie horror hit, *Five Nights at Freddy's*, which deals with homicidal animatronics who come to life during the night shift at a family restaurant, is in the early stages of development.

Tom Holland as Nathan Drake in *Uncharted* – © Sony Pictures Releasing

The sequel to 2018's *Tomb Raider* will continue the adventures of Alicia Vikander's Lara Croft, and a *Tomb Raider* anime series that follows the rebooted video game trilogy continuity will come to Netflix in the future. *Castlevania* wrapped with its fourth season for Netflix in 2021, but spin-off series are in development, with new characters.

Other forthcoming projects include an adaptation of *Tom Clancy's The Division,* and, of course, the animated version of *Super Mario Bros.* from Illumination. It will release in December 2022 and features an all-star voice cast, including Chris Pratt as Mario, Charlie Day as Luigi, Jack Black as Bowser, and Anya Taylor-Joy as Peach, among many other prolific actors and comedians. The man behind Mario's voice for three decades, Charles Martinet, will also feature in the film. A sequel to the hit *Detective Pikachu* also seems to be on the cards.

Video games continue their journey on television too, with a series based on *Halo* satisfying fans' need for Covenant-blasting action. Amazon are working with *Westworld* team Lisa Joy and Jonathan Nolan to adapt the apocalyptic open-world series *Fallout* for television. A massively ambitious production of Naughty Dog's *The Last of Us* series is on the way from the game's creator, Neil Druckmann, and Craig Mazin, who brought the immensely popular *Chernobyl* to our screens. Joel and Ellie, the game series' protagonists, will be played by Pedro Pascal (*The Mandalorian, Game of Thrones*) and Bella Ramsey (*Game of Thrones*) respectively.

Hideo Kojima's highly-successful and influential espionage series *Metal Gear Solid* will be given the long-awaited big-screen treatment by *Kong: Skull Island* director Jordan Vogt-Roberts.

From the first-person looter shooter *Borderlands* - which will be led by Kevin Hart and Cate Blanchett, along with comedian and musician Jack Black lending his voice to the robot Claptrap - to the global phenomenon *Minecraft*, there's bound to be something for all gamers and viewers alike in the next 30 years of games on film.